Volume 7 CONTENTS

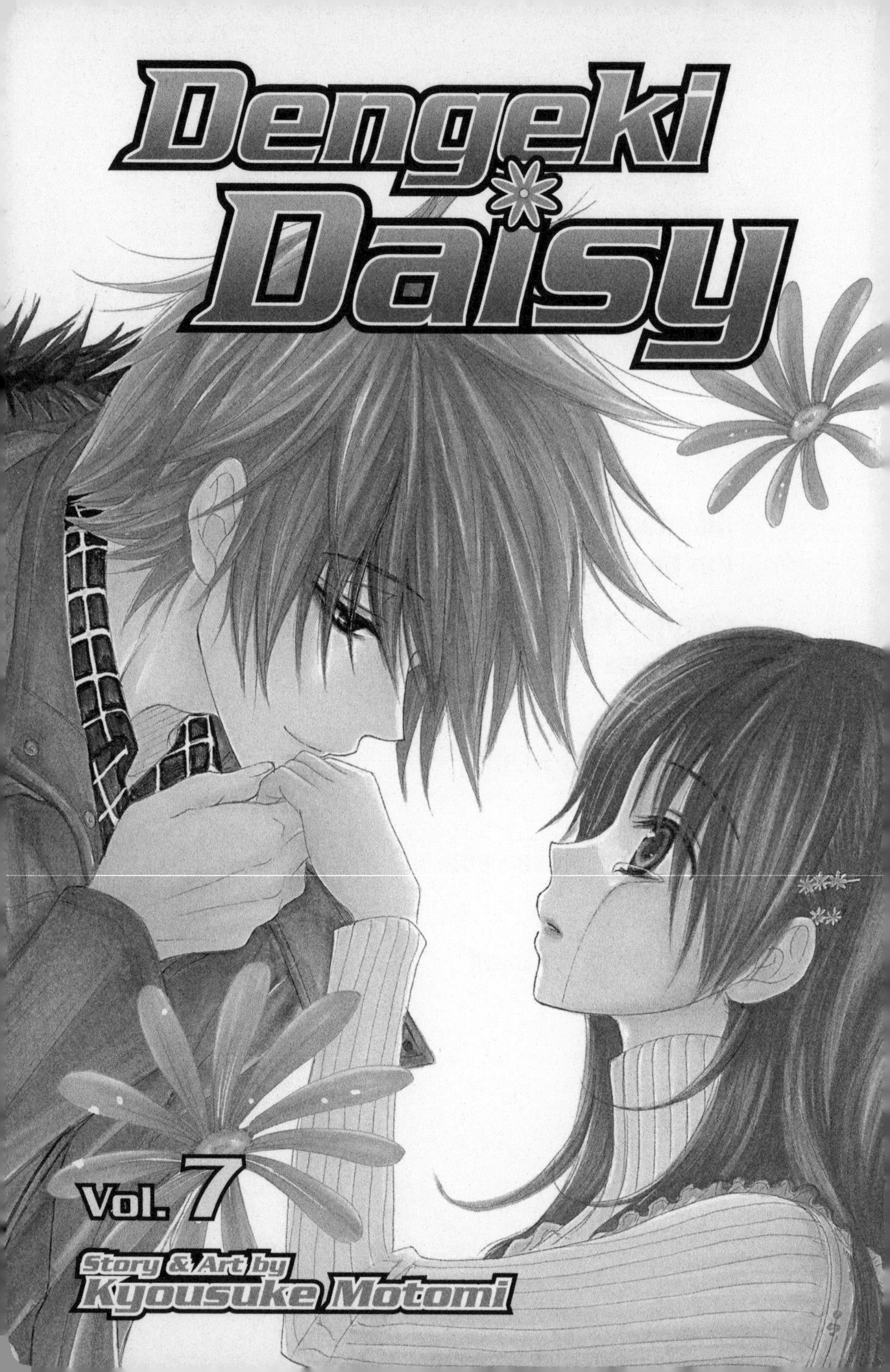
Dengeki Daisy
Vol. 7
Story & Art by
Kyousuke Motomi

Dengeki Daisy Vol. 7

★ Tasuku Kurosaki ★
Continues to protect Teru as "Daisy." "Daisy" is his handle from his days as a hacker. He is in love with Teru.

★ Teru Kurebayashi ★
Although she is poor and has no living relatives, Teru remains positive and true to herself. A second-year high school student, she has deep feelings for Kurosaki.

★ After losing her brother, the only living relative she had, Teru's sole consolation was the cell phone he left her because she received messages from a mysterious person known only as "Daisy" on it. Whatever hardships she faced, Teru was able to endure them because of the encouragement these messages gave her.

★ One day, Teru accidentally breaks a window at school. To pay for it, she ends up becoming a servant for Kurosaki, the delinquent school custodian. Although he is brusque and works her like a slave, Kurosaki is always there in her time of need, and Teru finds herself increasingly drawn to him.

★ By chance, Teru discovers that Kurosaki is actually Daisy. Thinking that there must be a reason why Kurosaki has chosen to hide his identity, Teru decides to keep this knowledge to herself.

CHARACTERS...

★ Chiharu Mori ★
She used to work at Teru's school and was the perpetrator behind the fake Daisy incident.

★ Rena ★
Teru's friend. She once was romantically involved with Arai.

★ Kiyoshi Hasegawa ★
Teru's friend since grade school and Kurosaki's number two servant.

★ Soichiro Kurebayashi ★
Teru's older brother and a genius systems engineer. He died after leaving Teru in Kurosaki's care.

★ Arai ★
Arai used to be a teacher at Teru's school. He became embroiled in the fake Daisy incident.

★ Takeda ★
Soichiro's former coworker. He is the owner of Kaoruko, a Shiba dog.

★ Director (Kazumasa Ando) ★
He used to work with Soichiro and is currently the director of Teru's school.

★ Riko Onizuka ★
She was Soichiro's girlfriend and is now a counselor at Teru's school.

STORY...

★ One day, an email virus supposedly sent by Daisy spreads throughout the school. Kurosaki is determined to uncover this fake Daisy, but he is injured while trying to protect Teru from an unknown assailant.

★ Teru vows to stay close to Kurosaki after he saves her life. Meanwhile, Kurosaki begins to realize that in order to be with Teru, he will have to disclose the truth.

★ As the fake Daisy incident nears its climax, we discover that the real culprit behind it is Chiharu Mori, the school nurse and health teacher. Although she manages to escape, peaceful days somehow return to Teru's and Kurosaki's lives...?

CHAPTER 30: I'M THE ONLY ONE WHO KNOWS

HELLO, EVERYONE!!! IT'S KYOUSUKE MOTOMI.

DENGEKI DAISY IS AT VOLUME 7, YOU GUYS!!

SEVEN. AS IN "LUCKY SEVEN."

I HOPE YOU ENJOY IT.

PLEASE, PLEASE DON'T STOP READING UNTIL THE VERY LAST PAGE.

THANK YOU VERY MUCH.

I mentioned this in volume 6, but the blue daisies in my yard are blooming like crazy. I have no clue how to take care of them, like pruning or fertilizing. If anyone knows, please tell me...

WHAT WAS THAT SOUND?
HUH? WHAT SOUND?
IT WAS LIKE A SMALL BALLOON POPPING...
WHAT ARE YOU TALKING ABOUT? WHAT SMALL BALLOON ...?
Ah...
NHH...
HIHCHU!
UGH, MY NOSE IS ALL STUFFY...
HEY, WHAT'S THE MATTER?
TWCH TWCH
TWCH
KUROSAKI ACTUALLY LAUGHS QUITE A LOT.
BWA HA HA HA HA HA! WHAT THE HELL WAS THAT? DID YOU JUST SNEEZE?!
HYA HA HA HA HA!
HA HA HA HA!
Y-YEAH. WHY? WHAT'S WRONG WITH MY SNEEZE?
IT'S NOT FUNNY!! YOU'RE BEING RUDE!
SORRY, I COULDN'T HELP MYSELF. I MEAN... HA HA HA...

TASUKU KUROSAKI, SCHOOL CUSTODIAN.
HIS HAIR'S BLEACHED BLOND, HE'S A HEAVY SMOKER, AND HE'S GOT A MEAN LOOK TO HIM.
AT FIRST GLANCE, YOU'D THINK HE'S THE NOT-TOO-BRIGHT DELINQUENT TYPE.
Just how long are you going to keep laughing, you...! You...!
Ha ha... Ha...
Oh man, I can't stop...
THE TRUTH IS, HE'S A SKILLED HACKER CALLED DAISY.
Heh heh... Now my stomach hurts...
AND I'M ONE OF ONLY A FEW PEOPLE WHO KNOW THIS.

AH, THAT WAS A GOOD LAUGH. SORRY.
WELL, SERVANT, YOU DID A GOOD JOB.
LET'S CALL IT A DAY.
YOU HAVE EXAMS SOON, RIGHT? DON'T WORK DURING TEST TIME.
OH, YOU KNOW ABOUT THE EXAMS?
YEAH, WHO DOESN'T ?
HE LAUGHS EASILY, AND ALTHOUGH HE TALKS ROUGH, HE CAN BE KIND.
THOSE SNEEZES MIGHT BE THE START OF A COLD.
TAKE CARE OF YOUR-SELF, WILL YA?
I'VE GOT A LOT TO DO BEFORE THE WEATHER TURNS COLD.
I GUESS I SHOULDN'T FOOL AROUND THE ENTIRE YEAR.
KURO-SAKI, ARE YOU WORKING LATE AGAIN?
YOU'VE BEEN BUSY RECENT-LY.
CHAK
YEAH, WELL...
DESPITE HIS WORDS...
...HE WORKS (?) QUITE DILIGENT-LY.

Well, I'll help wash the mop at least.
THIS IS THE KUROSAKI ONLY I KNOW.
Ah, how thoughtful of you. I'm impressed.
IT MAKES ME HAPPY KNOWING THAT I'M THE ONLY ONE WHO SEES THIS SIDE OF HIM.
STILL, A PART OF ME WISHES THAT OTHER PEOPLE KNEW THE TRUTH...
WHAT PEOPLE THINK OF KUROSAKI ...?
ACTUALLY, QUITE A FEW TEACHERS LIKE HIM.
OH, REALLY?
SHING
ESPECIALLY THE TEACHERS WHO TEACH PRACTICAL SUBJECTS AND THOSE WHO SMOKE.
THEY FIND HIM USEFUL.
HE CREATED A SMOKING SECTION ON A LOW BUDGET FOR US.
I have nothing bad to say about him.
STUDENTS FEAR HIM, SO TRUANCY AND SCHOOL VIOLATIONS HAVE GONE DOWN.
KEIGO SHIBUZAWA (48, TEACHES P.E.)
HE MAY NOT LOOK IT, BUT HE'S QUITE HELPFUL. I HAVE NO COM-PLAINTS.
MINORU AIHARA (55, TEACHES CLASSICAL LITERATURE)

HMM... NO KIDDING.
They all have their reasons, huh?
WHAT'S MORE INTEREST-ING IS THE REACTION OLDER FEMALE TEACHERS HAVE.
THEY'RE HUGE FANS OF HIS.
HE'S A FINE YOUNG MAN. I MEAN IT.
PEOPLE MISJUDGE HIM BECAUSE OF HIS LOOKS.
But I'm a staunch sup-porter.
KIYOMI SAKURAMOTO (50, TEACHES MUSIC)
HE'S ALWAYS CHEERFUL AND POLITE.
Good morning, Ms. Sakuramoto.
Oh, did you change your hairstyle?
Oh, my...
GOOD SOCIAL SKILLS
AND EVEN HIS BLOND HAIR...
OH... THIS IS MY NATURAL HAIR COLOR.
I know it causes a lot of talk.
I'M ACTUALLY PART BRITISH...
I DON'T WANT IT GETTING AROUND, SO PLEASE DON'T SAY ANYTHING.
IS HE CRAZY?
Go eat a scone or some-thing!
WHAT'S THE HARM? SHE BELIEVES IT.
HEH
HEH
And besides, it could be true.
STILL, I'M RELIEVED THAT HE HAS ALLIES.
I GUESS HE'S BEEN DOING WELL.
A FEW OF THE TEACHERS LIKE HIM...
...BUT MANY STILL CONSIDER HIM A LOSER.

For example...
TEACHERS WHO ARE PASSIONATE ABOUT THEIR WORK OR—
KURE-BAYASHI!
I HEARD YOU WERE IN THE HOSPITAL, SO I WAS WORRIED.
YOU SEEM WELL. THANK GOOD-NESS FOR THAT.
OH... MR. EGAWA.
KENJI EGAWA (25, TEACHES ENGLISH)
I HAVE SOMETHING IMPORTANT TO DISCUSS.
CAN YOU COME WITH ME TO THE OFFICE?
SURE...
THOSE WHO DON'T THINK HIGHLY OF KUROSAKI ARE TEACHERS LIKE MR. EGAWA...
...WHO LIKE TERU BECAUSE SHE'S A SMART HONOR STUDENT...
ENGLISH OFFICE B

MR. EGAWA, THESE ARE ANSWER SHEETS FOR THE QUIZZES.
YES, YOU MISSED TWO OF THEM.
Quiz (2-4)
JUST FILL THOSE OUT AND TURN THEM IN AS SOON AS YOU CAN.
FINALS ARE COMING UP, RIGHT?
QUIZ SCORES COUNT FOR HALF YOUR GRADE, SO I'LL NEED TO ADD THEM IN.
OH, I'M AWARE OF THAT.
BUT THIS WOULDN'T BE FAIR...
EVEN IF YOU TOOK THE QUIZZES WITH THE CLASS, YOU'D HAVE SCORED PERFECT ANYWAY.
BESIDES, YOU DON'T WANT TO RISK LOSING YOUR TOP STUDENT RANKING, DO YOU?
I HATE TO SAY THIS, BUT...
NO... I MEAN, THIS KIND OF SPECIAL TREATMENT ISN'T NECESSARY.
...TEACHERS LIKE HIM ARE THE CAUSE OF THE BULLYING I ENDURE SOMETIMES.
CAN I TAKE A TIMED MAKE-UP QUIZ?
I did miss class, after all.
OTHERWISE, NEVER MIND ABOUT THE QUIZ SCORES.
...
WHAT'S COME OVER YOU, KUREBAYASHI? YOU'VE BECOME QUITE OUTSPOKEN LATELY.
THAT'S NOT TRUE. I'VE ALWAYS BEEN...
YOU'VE BEEN ABSENT MORE OFTEN TOO. MAYBE YOUR SOCIAL LIFE HAS SOMETHING TO DO WITH THIS.

YOU'VE BEEN CHUMMY WITH THAT BLEACH-HEAD CUSTODIAN KUROSAKI FOR A WHILE NOW, RIGHT?
MAYBE HE'S A BAD INFLUENCE ON YOU?
SO THAT'S IT.
ARE YOU TWO DATING?
NO, NO, NO SUCH THING!!
WE JUST LIVE CLOSE TO EACH OTHER, AND...
DESPER-ATE
JUST KIDDING. I WOULDN'T THINK SUCH A THING.
YOU'RE NOT SEXY. GUYS JUST DON'T GO FOR YOU.
I DON'T MEAN THAT IN A BAD WAY.
Ha ha ha... Don't look so shocked.
I'M JUST NOT WORRIED ABOUT YOU IN THAT SENSE.
SERI-OUSLY, DON'T TAKE IT THE WRONG WAY.
YOU JERK.
That's hardly a compliment.

BUT KURE-BAYASHI...
AS YOUR TEACHER, I DON'T THINK IT'S A GOOD IDEA...
...FOR YOU TO BE ASSOCIA-TING WITH THAT KIND OF GUY.
I HATE TO BE BLUNT, BUT HE'S JUST AN UNEDUCATED DELINQUENT.
YOU CAN GUESS HIS WORTH JUST BY LOOKING AT HIS BLEACHED HAIR.
THAT'S NOT TRUE. HE'S A GOOD PERSON.
IF YOU GOT TO KNOW HIM, MR. EGAWA ...
WHAT'S THE POINT?
OH BOY, HE'S ALREADY GOT YOU FOOLED.
I HOPE YOU DON'T BELIEVE HIS NONSENSE ABOUT BEING PART BRITISH?
He convinced a few of our older female teachers, but...
I MEAN, HAVE YOU EVER HEARD HIM SPEAK ENGLISH?
YAK
YAK
YAK
YAK
...
I GUESS INNOCENT GIRLS ARE EASILY IN-FLUENCED.
WHAT'S HE TRYING TO TELL ME?
THE DAY YOU BLEACH YOUR OWN HAIR PROBABLY ISN'T FAR OFF.
I SHOULD HAVE TALKED TO YOU SOONER.

HE KEEPS RAMBLING ON AND ON...
IF YOUR SCORES DROP ON THE EXAMS, IT'LL BE THAT BLEACH-HEAD'S...
...ABOUT BLEACHED HAIR...
I UNDER-STAND.
I PROMISE MY GRADES WON'T DROP.
I WILL BE NUMBER ONE WITHOUT FAIL.
I won't take the make-up quizzes either. Call it a handicap.
LOOOOM
IF I DO DROP FROM NUMBER ONE...
...KUROSAKI'S BLEACHED HAIR WILL—

What ?!
SHE'S GONNA ASK HIM TO DYE HIS HAIR?
No way. Are you serious?
YUP, IF SHE'S NO LONGER TOP OF THE CLASS.
I can't believe she made such a bet.
ONLY NOW, SHE'S CRAMMING.
I COULDN'T BRING MYSELF TO SAY THAT HE'D *SHAVE* HIS HEAD.
MMBL MMBL
But I had to stand my ground and say something.
THERE'S A HUGE PROBLEM WITH ALL THIS, THOUGH.
You have a nosebleed.
YOU DIDN'T ASK KUROSAKI, DID YOU?
I sure won't do it.
B-BUT IT'LL BE OKAY.
Heh heh. I haven't been at the top of the class all these years for nothing.
SNIFF
I JUST HAVE TO BE NUMBER ONE AGAIN. THEN DYEING HIS HAIR WILL BE A NON-ISSUE.
THAT KIND OF OPTIMISM ALWAYS ENDS IN FAILURE.
Besides, your top grades have been nothing short of a miracle.
SHOCK
HEY, WAIT A MINUTE.
IF YOU DON'T MAKE IT TO THE TOP OF THE CLASS...

...KURO-SAKI WILL HAVE TO...
...DYE HIS HAIR BLACK ...
HMM... I CAN TOTALLY PICTURE IT.
He'd look cool.
The heroes in shojo manga always have black hair.
HE'D LOOK MORE CONSER-VATIVE THOUGH ...
WELL, THAT MAY NOT BE A BAD THING.
I THINK HE SHOULD DYE HIS HAIR BLACK TOO.
TO BE HONEST, I THINK HE AND I LOOK TOO MUCH ALIKE!
DOOOM
THEN HE'LL BE MORE LIKE ME...
I'm cool with that. I'm an open-minded guy.
Two birds of a feather.
DO YOU HEAR WHAT YOU'RE SAYING?
Look in the mirror.
KIYOSHI
STILL, IT'S A GOOD OPPOR-TUNITY.
I DON'T CARE FOR MR. EGAWA...
...BUT I AGREE THAT IT'S INAPPROPRIATE FOR A GROWN-UP TO BLEACH HIS HAIR LIKE THAT.
He's only allowed to because of the school's good graces.
ALL RIGHT, TERU! DON'T STUDY AT ALL !!!
WHAT THE HELL?! NO ONE'S ON MY SIDE!
Kiyoshi, hide her notes!
Roger that.

I MUST SAVE KUROSAKI'S BLEACHED HAIR!
KUROSAKI, DO YOU HAVE A MINUTE?
WHAT IS IT, MR. EGAWA?
Sorry to bother you.
THAT BOX I ASKED YOU TO DUMP...
CAN WE CHECK WHAT'S INSIDE?
OH, I FOUND IT. THANK GOOD-NESS.
CONFIDENTIAL
THIS IS A SENSITIVE DOCUMENT THAT SHOULD BE SHREDDED.
Well, it's my mistake.
IT WAS AT THE TOP OF THE STACK, AND IT SAYS SO RIGHT HERE IN ENGLISH.
I WISH YOU HAD NOTICED.
I'M SORRY. I DIDN'T LOOK INSIDE.
It's trash, after all.
IS THAT RIGHT?

HEH HEH
OR MAYBE YOU COULDN'T UNDER-STAND THE ENGLISH?
THAT'S STRANGE.
I HEARD SOMEWHERE THAT YOU'RE PART BRITISH.
HA HA. WHO TOLD YOU THAT? SORRY, THAT'S NOT TRUE.
I'M NOT BRITISH.
HA HA HA
I used that line to win over the older female teachers.
OF COURSE, I SAW RIGHT THROUGH IT.
HA HA HA HA
IT'S RATHER SILLY TO TELL THAT LIE. OR TO BELIEVE IT. I MEAN WELL, OF COURSE.
BY THE WAY, DID KURE-BAYASHI TELL YOU?
HUH?
IF SHE DOESN'T FINISH FIRST IN HER EXAMS...
...SHE'S GOING TO HAVE YOU DYE YOUR HAIR BLACK.
NO KIDDING? WELL, IT'S NO BIG DEAL.
BUT WHAT BROUGHT THAT ON?
OH, SHE GOT CARRIED AWAY DURING OUR DISCUS-SION.
I WAS QUITE SHOCKED AT HOW MUCH SHE ADORES YOU.

KUROSAKI, I'D LIKE YOU TO DO ONE MORE THING.
IF KUREBAYASHI DOESN'T MAKE IT TO THE TOP OF HER CLASS...
...I'D LIKE YOU TO CUT ALL TIES WITH HER.
I'M SORRY TO PUT IT SO BLUNTLY, BUT YOU'RE NOT A SUITABLE ROLE MODEL.
AND IT'S MY DUTY AS A TEACHER TO PROTECT MY STUDENTS.
GIFTED STUDENTS NEED TO BE NURTURED IN THE BEST POSSIBLE ENVIRON-MENT.
Look! Here's the latest issue!
BETSUCOMI
DO YOU THINK I'M BEING UN-REASON-ABLE?
YOU OBVIOUSLY DON'T THINK SO.
AND YOU CONSIDER YOURSELF A GOOD ROLE MODEL...
You sure are confident.
OF COURSE! AT THE VERY LEAST, I'M A BETTER ROLE MODEL THAN YOU ARE.
I don't mean that in a bad way!
POINT

WELL, THAT'S ALL I HAVE TO SAY.
WE HAVE AN AGREEMENT THEN. PLEASE DON'T FORGET!
...
I didn't agree to anything.
OH WELL, WHATEVER.
SAY, MR. EGAWA...
WHAT IS IT? WE'RE DONE TALKING...
IT'S ABOUT ANOTHER MATTER. NOTHING IMPORTANT, REALLY.
IS THE COMPUTER YOU'RE USING IN OFFICE B...
...RUNNING PROPERLY?
YES. I HAVEN'T NOTICED ANYTHING WRONG.
GOTCHA.
HEY, YOU EVER HEARD OF A HACKER NAMED DAISY?
WHAT IS THIS ABOUT?
I've heard rumors...
TWTCH

IF SOMETHING COMES UP, ASK TERU KUREBAYASHI.
I UNDERSTAND THIS DAISY...
...ONLY LISTENS TO THAT GIRL'S REQUESTS.
LIBRARY
...HIH-CHU!
...HIH-CHU!!
...CHOO!

AGH...
Was that a sneeze just now?
Shh...
...
PFFT
YOU DON'T LOOK SO GOOD, TERU.
DID YOU PULL AN ALL-NIGHTER AGAIN?
SNFF
YEAH. I FEEL A COLD COMING ON.
BUT I HAVE TO KEEP GOING. OTHERWISE, KUROSAKI WILL BE FORCED TO... NO!!
I made this bet, and I'm going to win!!
SKRCH SKRCH
LOSING MEANS SUBMITTING TO EGAWA'S "KUROSAKI IS WORTHLESS" THEORY.
You've got a runny nose and a nosebleed now.
I DON'T AGREE WITH YOU. AT LEAST, NOT THIS TIME.
YOU SHOULDN'T TAKE IT SO PERSON-ALLY.
I'm going home.
JUST DON'T OVERDO IT. TOMORROW'S THE EXAM.
YOU DON'T WANT TO GET SICK.
PAT PAT
HE'S RIGHT.
I *AM* TAKING IT PERSON-ALLY.
SNFF

DENGEKI DAISY QUESTION CORNER
BALDLY ASK!!
...HI! I'VE BROUGHT YOU THIS CORNER WHERE I ASK FOR YOUR KINDNESS AND UNDERSTANDING. I'LL GIVE PRIORITY TO HUMOROUS QUESTIONS AND REPLY TO AS MANY AS POSSIBLE.
PLEASE READ THIS WITH AN OPEN MIND. HERE WE GO!!!
Q.
HERE'S A QUESTION FOR DAISY.
MY COMPUTER IS TURNED OFF, BUT ONCE IN A WHILE, IT TRIES TO START UP ON ITS OWN. IS THIS BAD? AND WHY DOES IT HAPPEN?
PLEASE TELL ME.
(KOUME, AICHI PREFECTURE)
A.
...TH-TH-THAT'S BAD... I-IT'S NOT GOOD TO ASK SUCH A SERIOUS QUESTION IN THIS SILLY CORNER. I ASKED DAISY, AND HE MENTIONED SOMETHING ABOUT A POSSIBLE SETTING IN "BIOS" OR SOMETHING. BUT I (THE AUTHOR) HAVE NO IDEA WHAT THIS MEANS BECAUSE I'M DUMB. PLEASE CONTACT AN I.T. SUPPORT SERVICE OR FIND SOMEONE WHO IS SMART AND KNOWLEDGEABLE!!!!! FOR THE TIME BEING, THIS DOESN'T LOOK LIKE IT'S A RESULT OF DAISY'S HACKING!!
I'M SORRY I WASN'T MUCH HELP... (BOW)
THIS TYPE OF QUESTION IS FORBIDDEN!! 'CAUSE I'LL CRY!!!
BUT...
I FINALLY FINISHED THE EXAM QUESTIONS.
Sorry.
YOU BARELY SUBMITTED THEM IN TIME.
MAKE SURE YOU PRINT THEM OUT.
SHEESH, WHAT'S THE BIG DEAL? I'LL GET IT DONE.
What an old biddy...
I JUST NEED TO OPEN THE FILE AND PRINT IT OUT.
Easy stuff.
BUT BEFORE THAT...
NICE, IT FINISHED DOWNLOADING.
I'M SO GLAD I GOT THIS NEW SOFTWARE FOR FREE.
DOWNLOAD COMPLETE

I've been wanting to see this movie...
I CAN'T WAIT TO CHECK IT OUT AT HOME TONIGHT.
IT'LL BE A NICE TREAT AFTER WORKING OVERTIME.
KLICK
FLASH
GASP...
?!
...?!
BEEP
02:59:54
PASSWORD:
BEEP
BEEP
BEEP
W-WHAT'S GOING ON?!
HEY, IT'S ANDY.
DO YOU HAVE A MINUTE? IT'S URGENT.
ACTUALLY, I DON'T. BUT WHAT'S UP?
I'm working.
I WAS MONITORING ACTIVITY ON THE SCHOOL'S NETWORK...

...AND IT LOOKS LIKE MR. EGAWA'S COMPUTER HAS BEEN HIT WITH A VIRUS.
LUCKILY, THE OTHER COMPUTERS DON'T SEEM TO BE AFFECTED ...
HMM... THAT'S GOOD.
IT'S NOT MY PROBLEM THOUGH.
THE SCHOOL IS CLOS-ING.
ALL STUD-ENTS MUST LEAVE...
LIBRARY
AGH, MY HEAD IS STARTING TO HURT.
SNFF SNFF
THIS SUCKS ...
K-KURE-BAYASHI !
Mr. Egawa ...?
TMP TMP
CAN YOU HELP ME?
SOME-THING'S WRONG WITH MY COMPUTER. I HAVE TO FIX IT IMMEDIATE-LY.
WHAT? WHY ARE YOU ASKING ME? I DON'T KNOW WHAT TO DO.
YOU SHOULD ASK ONE OF THE OTHER TEACHERS.
ERR... WELL, I CAN'T.

COME ON, HELP ME OUT.
YOU CAN ASK THAT HACKER CALLED DAISY, RIGHT?
And keep this to yourself.
Secretly, of course.
THEN WE'LL FORGET ALL ABOUT THE OTHER DAY...
I DON'T THINK I SHOULD GET INVOLVED.
VWP
DAISY IS A RIGHTEOUS HACKER AND ONLY HELPS GOOD PEOPLE.
AHHH
WHAT?! OH, COME ON... EVERYONE NEEDS HELP SOME-TIMES!
I-I'M IN A TIGHT SPOT... HEY...
OKAY! LOOK, I'M SORRY! I'M SORRY!
SERVES YOU RIGHT.
THAT'S WHAT YOU GET FOR ACTING SO SMUG AND CRITICIZING KUROSAKI.
LOOK, I REALLY NEED YOUR HELP! PLEASE!
NO WAY AM I GONNA HELP YOU.

PLEASE ...!!
WHY SHOULD I?
WELL, I GUESS THIS IS ONE TIME...
...EVEN A GOODY TWO-SHOES...

...CAN'T DO A THING.
Date: ----/--/--
From: Teru_K
Title: Please help
Hi Daisy,
My teacher Mr. Egawa is having trouble with his computer. Please help him.
THAT TEACHER'S PET...
HIHCHU...
HIHCHU!
I'M ALWAYS...
I'M SORRY, KURO-SAKI...
OH, KURO-SAKI... YOU'RE STILL HERE?
Thank good-ness.
WHAT'S UP, TERU?
You're sneezing a lot.
...RELY-ING ON HIM.
I...

WHY'RE YOU SORRY?
BECAUSE I HAVE TO DYE MY HAIR BLACK IF YOU'RE NOT NUMBER ONE?
?!!
TWCH
Y-YOU KNOW ABOUT THAT? HOW...?
MR. EGAWA TOLD ME. FUNNY GUY. I DON'T MEAN THAT IN A *BAD* WAY.
...
HOW DID THIS COME ABOUT ANYWAY? TELL ME. I WON'T GET UPSET.
Too upset.
DONG
DONG
I'M SORRY... IT'S SO STUPID.
I should have just ignored him...
I LET HIM UPSET ME...
HE SAID YOU'RE NO GOOD JUST BECAUSE YOU BLEACH YOUR HAIR.
HE SAID I SHOULDN'T ASSOCIATE WITH YOU...
Among other things...
BUT I SWEAR THAT WON'T HAPPEN!
I mean having you dye your hair black.
I'LL BE NUMBER ONE IN CLASS! I'LL HIT THE BOOKS SOME MORE TONIGHT AND...
TUG

DONG
DONG

LOOKS LIKE YOU HAVE A SLIGHT...
...FEVER.

HUH? WHAT?
GO HOME AND EAT SOMETHING, THEN GO STRAIGHT TO BED.
I FORBID YOU FROM STUDYING ANY MORE TONIGHT.
BUT I HAVE TO STUDY...
NOPE. YOU'VE STUDIED ENOUGH.
Or you'll have to...
IF I HAVE TO DYE MY HAIR BLACK, I WILL.
BUT IF YOU FLUNK YOUR TESTS BECAUSE YOU'RE TOO SICK...
...THEN I'LL DYE YOUR HAIR RED AND PERM IT SO THAT IT'S FRIZZY. YA GOT THAT?!
EEEE
Y-YES, SIR. I'LL GO HOME RIGHT NOW AND TAKE CARE OF MYSELF!!
Please forgive me.
Oh no, it's dark already.
"...I'D LIKE YOU TO CUT ALL TIES WITH HER.
"...IT'S MY DUTY AS A TEACHER TO PROTECT MY STUDENTS."
HMPH...

DON'T COUNT ON IT.
AS IF I'D LET HER GO.
THANK YOU, KUROSAKI.
YOU'RE SO KIND...
Hihchu!
I'M PROBABLY THE ONLY ONE...
...WHO KNOWS THIS SIDE OF YOU.
ENGLISH OFFICE B
DAMMIT... I CAN'T ACCESS MY FILES FROM THE OTHER COMPUTERS.
AND IT'S TOO LATE TO MAKE ANOTHER EXAM...
IF THE SCHOOL FINDS OUT MY COMPUTER'S INFECTED...
<Come on, Mantis...>
?
<I know you did it.>

<Your virus infected my co-worker's computer.>
<It's going to crash in ten minutes. You really go overboard, man.>
00:10:29
<Just tell me, for God's sake. This is a real hassle for me.>
<...Of course. That's so typical of you.>
<Don't goof around too much. See ya.>
HUH?! WHA ...?!
YOU'RE IN LUCK, MR. EGAWA.
You...
I HAPPEN TO KNOW THE GUY WHO CREATED THIS CRAPPY VIRUS.
TAP TAP TAP...
THIS COMPUTER IS SET TO LOSE EVERYTHING IN THREE HOURS, BUT THERE'S A PASSWORD TO STOP IT...
PASSWORD ?
All the world's a stage,
And all the men and women me
They have their exits and their entr
nd one man in his time plays many parts,
ts being seven ages.
WHAT KIND OF SADIST COMES UP WITH A PASSWORD LIKE THIS?
I mean, Shakespeare?
YOU WIN

OKAY, IT'S FIXED. LUCKY, HUH?
I'm off.
VRRR
This is way too suspicious!!
HOLD IT RIGHT THERE!
YOU WERE SPEAKING FLUENT ENGLISH JUST NOW!
DON'T TELL ME YOU ACTUALLY HAVE...
...British blood?
WHY THE SURPRISED LOOK? IT'S JUST CONVER-SATIONAL ENGLISH.
Blood has nothing to do with language ability.
BESIDES, YOU SHOULD BE SURPRISED ABOUT SOMETHING ELSE ENTIRELY.
WHO DO YOU THINK REALLY CAME TO YOUR RESCUE?
WRRR
WE BOTH WANT TO KEEP THIS A SECRET, RIGHT?
SO WE SHOULD BE FRIENDS. I DON'T MEAN THAT IN A BAD WAY.
RIGHT...
OH, AND ABOUT TERU KURE-BAYASHI.

I PROBABLY KNOW THE REAL KUROSAKI ...
Daisy
Dear Teru, I took care of Mr. Egawa's problem. You don't have to worry about him anymore. Have a good night's sleep.
THERE'S NO NEED FOR YOU TO WORRY.
I'LL TAKE GOOD CARE OF HER.
...BETTER THAN ANYONE ELSE...

ANYWAY, AMIDST ALL THIS...
...EXAM DAY CAME. AND IN THE END...
...I CAME IN NUMBER ONE, FAR BEYOND ANYONE ELSE.
I actually studied much harder than usual.
ALSO, GETTING A FULL NIGHT'S REST CERTAINLY DIDN'T HURT.
FWEF FWEF
BOO
BOO
BOO BOO
BOO
ONLOOKERS BOOED LIKE CRAZY.
MR. EGAWA SUDDENLY BEGAN TO AVOID ME.
Oh, you're looking well. I don't mean that in a bad way.
See you.
?
I MEAN IN A WEIRD WAY.
AND JUST AS YOU'D EXPECT...
...KURO-SAKI REMAINED A BLEACHED-BLOND DELIN-QUENT.
And I'm still his servant.
...

I AM A LITTLE CURIOUS ABOUT HOW HE'D LOOK WITH DARK HAIR THOUGH...
HEY, KUROSAKI, WHY DO YOU BLEACH YOUR HAIR?
I hope you're grateful that I saved it.
IS IT BECAUSE YOU THINK IT'S COOL?
MAYBE I DO IT BECAUSE I'M...
... LAZY.
WHAT? IF YOU'RE LAZY, THEN WHY BOTHER BLEACHING IT?
YOU SHOULD JUST SHAVE IT ALL OFF!
A buzz cut! That's the easiest!
...
BUT I THINK HE LOOKS BEST WITH BLEACHED HAIR.

CHAPTER 31: WHAT WAS TAKEN FROM ME

FWAP
SHA...

Hello. It's a nice day today, isn't it?
Have an orange. It has lots of vitamins, you know. Take care of yourself, okay?
Yay, thanks!
JIGGLE♡
Kurosaki seems to like this teacher a lot.

THE OLDER FEMALE TEACHER IN CHAPTER 30, KIYOMI SAKURAMOTO, IS NOT THE OLDER WOMAN WHO APPEARED IN VOLUME 1, CHAPTER 2 (THE ONE WHO BUMPED TERU WITH HER BIG BUTT). WHENEVER I TRY TO DRAW MATURE WOMEN WITH BIG BUTTS, THEY END UP LOOKING LIKE HER. BASED ON REAL-LIFE INTERACTIONS, I THINK THAT MATURE WOMEN WHO HAVE BIG BUTTS LIKE THIS CAN NEVER BE BAD PEOPLE. THE AUTHOR HOLDS TO THE THEORY THAT IN MOST CASES, THEIR HEARTS ARE BIGGER THAN THEIR BUTTS, AND THEY ARE GOOD WOMEN. WHAT DO YOU THINK?

BOY, YOUR GRAVE NEEDS ATTEN-TION.
SHA...
SOMEONE IMPORTANT LIKE YOU DESERVES BETTER.
NOT MANY PEOPLE COME OUT TO THE MOUNTAINS, HUH.
I MEAN, IT'S MY FIRST TIME HERE TOO...

YOU MAY NOT APPROVE...
...BUT I BROUGHT YOU SOME FLOWERS...
MIDOR
...PROFES-SOR.
KUROSAKI TOOK A HALF-DAY OFF AND WENT SOME-WHERE.
THAT WAS THE MORNING IT HAPPENED ...
IT'S GOTTEN SO COLD.
DID YOU PREP FOR CLASS, TERU?
HUH? YEAH...
SHUP

VSH
VROO...
VROOO
A YO-YO IN THIS DAY AND AGE?
And it's new too...
SHUP
HEY... IS HE THAT SAME GUY...
...FROM THE OTHER DAY?
"EXCUSE ME..."
"SAME HERE. SORRY!"
VRR...
WOOSH
OH...

EXCUSE ME...
Teru ...?
ARE'NT YOU GETTING ON THE BUS?
THANKS, BUT I'M FINE.
PAT
BUT YOU BETTER GET ON BEFORE IT LEAVES WITHOUT YOU.
SHUNK...
I THOUGHT SO...
SMILE
HE DOES LOOK LIKE HIM.
IT'S NOT MY IMAGINA-TION, RIGHT?

HE SMILED AT ME...
He seems nice.
Get your bus pass out.
WHAT'S WITH THAT SMILE ON YOUR FACE?
DID THAT GUY DO SOMETHING?
DIDN'T HE KINDA LOOK LIKE MY BROTHER?
HUH? DID HE?
I WAS HAPPY, THAT'S ALL.
BECAUSE IN A SMALL WAY...
...HE HAD PIQUED MY INTEREST...
AND WHAT WERE THE CHANCES OF RUNNING INTO HIM AGAIN?
♪
?
HUH? WAIT...
MY PASS...

GENERAL HOSPITAL
DESCRIBE AKIRA'S APPEARANCE? WELL...
SKRCH SKRCH
HE ALWAYS HAD A BASEBALL CAP OR A HOODIE ON, SO I DIDN'T GET A CLOSE LOOK AT HIS FACE...
...BUT I THINK HE HAS ALMOND-SHAPED EYES AND LONGISH BLACK HAIR...
AND HE'S ABOUT THE SAME HEIGHT AS YOU... ABOUT FIVE FOOT SEVEN...
SKRCH SKRCH
Have some of this.
PUDDING
THANK YOU FOR COOPERATING WITH US, MR. ARAI.
NO NEED TO THANK ME. I'M GLAD TO BE OF HELP.
I'm feeling much better now too.
ARE YOU GUYS DOING AN INVESTIGATION OF YOUR OWN?
NO, NOTHING LIKE THAT. WE'RE LEAVING MOST OF IT TO THE POLICE.
BUT WE DO WANT TO TAKE EVERY PRECAUTION.
WE WOULDN'T WANT TO BE CAUGHT UNAWARE.
AND WE CAN'T GO AROUND SUSPECTING EVERYONE...
This one's for me.
IT'S TOO BAD DRAWING A SKETCH OF HIM IS ABOUT ALL WE CAN DO.

IF THIS YOUNG MAN IS CHIHARU MORI'S ACCOMPLICE...
Hmm...
She could have been using him the same way she used you...
...WOULD HE RISK COMING HERE KNOWING THAT THE POLICE ARE WORKING ON THE CASE?
SURELY HE'S NOT THAT STUPID...
BUT WOULD HE COME *BECAUSE* HE THINKS WE BELIEVE THAT?
Nah, I'm reading too much into this.
ARAI, CAN YOU THINK OF ANYTHING ELSE ABOUT AKIRA?
LET'S SEE... HE'S SKINNY AND TENDS TO SLOUCH.
HE USES A SCOOTER TO GET AROUND.
ONCE IN A WHILE, HE'D HAVE THIS WIDE, TWISTED GRIN...
...AND...
...HE ALWAYS CARRIES A YO-YO. LIKE IT'S A COMFORTING THING TO HOLD...
HEY, WAIT A SEC...
SCRCH
DIRECTOR, WHO DOES THIS LOOK LIKE TO YOU?
THIS LOOKS LIKE...

...A DEMON.
· LONG HAIR
· HOOD OR CAP
TWISTED GRIN
· SKINNY
· ALMOND-SHAPPED EYES
SLOUCHES
· HOODIE OR JACKET
· 5'7"
SCOOTER
CERTAINLY NOT ANYTHING HUMAN. I'VE SEEN IT SOMEWHERE...
We can look it up.
NO, KUROSAKI, IT'S NOT BAD. MY DESCRIPTION WAS INADEQUATE.
REALLY, IT'S NOT BAD AT ALL. MAYBE I SHOULD TRY DRAWING IT?
PAT
TREMBLE
DONG
DONG
I ALMOST FORGOT, TERU.
THIS IS THAT BOOK ABOUT SECRET CODES THAT I WAS GOING TO LEND YOU—
KLAK KLAK
ARE YOU STILL DE-PRESSED?
I CAN'T BELIEVE I LOST MY BUS PASS...
I JUST RENEWED IT AND PAID 2000 YEN*...
MUMBLE
MUMBLE
MUMBLE
MUMBLE
I have to find it...

*ABOUT $24.60

TERU'S FORTUNE SAYS HER WEEK WILL BE FULL OF UPS AND DOWNS.
"IF YOU HAVE TYPE O BLOOD, YOU SHOULD BE ESPECIALLY CAREFUL WITH MONEY.
BEEP
"YOUR LOVE LIFE WILL BE ON THE STORMY SIDE TOO.
"AN UNEXPECTED ENCOUNTER WITH SOMEONE THAT INTERESTS YOU MAY BE THE CAUSE OF TROUBLE WITH YOUR LOVER.
"HONESTLY DISCUSS ISSUES YOU FEEL LIKE AVOIDING, AND THINGS WILL TAKE A TURN FOR THE BETTER... PERHAPS A FIRST XX?!
DRACULA'S BLOOD-TYPE FORTUNE
THIS WEEK'S WARNING: THE COLOR AND ALIGNMENT OF YOUR TEETH IS WORRISOME.
IF YOU HAVE TYPE O BLOOD YOU SHOULD BE ESPECIALLY CAREFUL
"YOUR LUCKY ITEM IS MILK. TO BUILD UP YOUR BUST.♡" THAT'S WHAT IT SAYS.
They say this fortune-teller is always right.
I DON'T BELIEVE SUCH FLIGHTY FORTUNES.
I mean, milk? In a fortune?
I think she's right.
Sounds pretty generic to me.
BESIDES, WHAT DOES HE MEAN BY "FIRST XX"? THAT'S SO VAGUE.
Per-haps... a first kiss? ♡
I'm Type O too. ♡
MMWAH
WHAT IS THAT SUPPOSED TO MEAN?
Don't tell me you and Ken kissed?
AH HA HA.♡ DID THAT SOUND LIKE I WAS BRAG-GING? I'M SORRY.
GAH
IT'S QUITE ACCURATE. BUT I'M JUST TALKING ABOUT ME.
WE WERE ON A DATE YESTERDAY, AND I MADE A CONFESSION TO HIM...
"KEN, I...
"I HAVE TO TELL YOU SOMETHING..."

I'M NOT REALLY AN E-CUP. I'M AN A-CUP...
But I knew you're partial to breasts, so...!
I'VE BEEN USING A PUSH-UP BRA EVEN BEFORE WE STARTED DATING...
I ALREADY KNOW THAT, SILLY.
DO NOT UNDER-ESTIMATE THE DISCERN-ING EYE OF THE MALE VIRGIN.
I haven't touched them yet, but I sized them up long ago.
YOUR CHEST IS EVER SO SLIGHTLY DIFFERENT EVERY DAY. I SENSED THAT FROM THE START.
LET ME MAKE THIS CLEAR, KAKO. I LOVE YOU.
TO-GETHER, WE'LL NURTURE...
...OUR LOVE—AND YOUR BOOBS.
OH, KEN... I LOVE YOU...
HOLD IT! SO DID THAT END WITH A KISS OR NOT?!
AHHH!♥
All you talked about was your boobs!
THERE'S SO MUCH I WANT TO SAY ABOUT THIS, BUT I DON'T EVEN KNOW WHERE TO BEGIN...!!!
HER REACTION WAS QUITE NORMAL.
HMM...
A KISS... THAT SOUNDS NICE...
Did you really kiss? If you did, his teeth would've left marks!!
Actually, that first kiss did taste like blood...
...!!!

TO BE HONEST, I HAVE THIS LONGING.
MOUTH-TO-MOUTH RESUSCITATION DOESN'T COUNT. BESIDES, I DON'T REMEMBER IT...
I WONDER WHAT A KISS FEELS LIKE.
MY LIPS TOUCHING...
...HIS LIPS.
I-I'M GOING HOME.
SHUP
SORRY, KIYOSHI. CAN YOU SEND KUROSAKI MY REGRETS?
Stop...

HUH? REGRETS ABOUT WHAT?
OH, JUST TELL HIM ANYTHING! AS SERVANT NUMBER 2!
I NEED TO LOOK FOR MY BUS PASS. BYE!!
Hey, the book...
GAAAH!!
IF I SEE HIM NOW, I'LL JUST ACT WEIRD!!
MY IMAGINATION TOTALLY RAN WILD. IT FELT SO REAL.
I MEAN, KUROSAKI AND ME... KISSING?
...
WILL IT HAPPEN?
WILL I...
...GET...
...KISSED?

DENGEKI DAISY QUESTION CORNER

BALDLY ASK!!

Q. DOES KUROSAKI WEAR VIRGINAL WHITE BRIEFS LIKE A YOUNG BOY? OR A PAIR OF TRUNKS? IN WHAT PATTERN? PLEASE TELL ME IN DETAIL!!!
(KYOUSUKE, SHIZUOKA PREFECTURE)

A. NOW THIS IS WHAT I CALL A GOOD, SILLY QUESTION. SORRY TO DISAPPOINT, BUT AT THIS TIME, KUROSAKI WEARS VERY BORING, AVERAGE BOXERS (IN GRAY OR BLACK). I OCCASIONALLY SPOT THEM (STICKING OUT FROM HIS WAIST). SORRY, THEY'RE BORING. BUT IF EVERYONE PASSIONATELY REQUESTS IT, MAYBE HE'LL CHANGE TO BRIEFS OR LEOPARD PRINTS OR EVEN THONGS. THAT'S IF YOU LIKE KUROSAKI LIKE THAT. BY THE WAY, KUROSAKI'S OWN PREFERENCE FOR TERU'S PANTIES IS WHITE. BABY BLUE OR PINK PANTIES AFTER THAT. HE'S YOUR AVERAGE PERVERTED MALE.

Q. WHAT'S THE FIRST THING TERU AND KUROSAKI DO WHEN THEY WAKE UP IN THE MORNING?
(KYOUSUKE, SHIZUOKA PREFECTURE)

A. TERU – ALWAYS WAKES UP REFRESHED, OPENS THE CURTAINS, THEN DOES SOME STRETCHING. ONCE IN A WHILE, SHE TURNS ON THE RADIO AND EXERCISES.
KUROSAKI – DUE TO HIS LOW BLOOD PRESSURE IN THE MORNING, HE'S SLOW TO GET UP. HE'LL START WITH A SHOWER, A DRINK OF WATER, AND A GRIN AT TERU'S PHOTO, AND HE WAKES UP SOMEHOW.
IT'S SOMETHING LIKE THAT. KYOUSUKE WHO SHARES THE SAME NAME AS ME (THE AUTHOR), THANK YOU FOR THE GREAT QUESTIONS!!

I ALREADY KNOW YOU AND THE DIRECTOR WENT TO THE HOSPITAL. I MEANT BEFORE THAT.
YEAH, I DID.
YOU TOOK A HALF-DAY OFF AND WENT SOME-WHERE, DIDN'T YOU?
I WENT TO PAY MY RESPECTS TO PROFESSOR MIDORIKAWA.
PROFES-SOR MIDORI-KAWA?
SORRY I DIDN'T TELL YOU... ARE YOU UPSET?
OH, STOP IT. OF COURSE NOT.
BUT IF I KNEW BEFORE-HAND, I WOULD'VE COME WITH YOU.
ANYWAY, I'LL GO ANOTHER TIME. SOMETIME SOON.
SO WHAT DID YOU DISCUSS WITH ARAI AT THE HOSPITAL?
OH... I WANTED TO GET MORE DETAILS ABOUT THIS AKIRA GUY...
KOFF KOFF...

OH, KIYOSHI.
What ...?
HI, THERE. IT'S JUST ME.
A-AM I INTERRUPTING? SORRY.
THAT'S ALL RIGHT. IT'S NOTHING SECRET.
I'M DONE FOR THE DAY, SO I'M HEADING HOME. SEE YOU.
OH, OKAY...
Have a good night.
I'M SORRY, I DIDN'T MEAN TO EAVESDROP.
Was that bad?
NO HARM DONE. IT WASN'T A SENSITIVE SUBJECT.
Stop looking so worried. It's okay.
SO WHY ARE YOU HERE? ACTING AS TERU'S GOFER OR SOMETHING?
Gofer?
YOU COULD SAY THAT... CAN YOU GIVE THIS BOOK TO HER?
Now you're the gofer.
TERU WENT HOME SO QUICKLY THAT I MISSED HER.
FWUP
SHE WANTS TO READ UP ON SECRET CODES, LIKE THE ONE I GAVE HER BEFORE.
I USED TO READ THIS MANUAL WHEN I WAS A KID.
OF THE FUTURE
SECRET COMPUTER CODES
By Hideo Midorikawa

IT'S A CHILDREN'S BOOK, BUT IT'S STILL GREAT.
SECRET COMPUTER CODES
IT'S EASY TO UNDERSTAND AND PRETTY INSPIRING... I TREASURE IT.
OH, I GET IT NOW. IS THAT WHY YOU GOT ALL EXCITED?
SO IT IS HIM? THIS AUTHOR IS THE SAME PROFESSOR YOU WERE TALKING ABOUT?!
THAT'S AMAZING! YOU KNOW HIM PERSONALLY? CAN YOU HELP ME GET ME HIS AUTOGRAPH?
Oh...
SORRY, THAT'S IMPOSSIBLE.
HE PASSED AWAY SEVERAL YEARS AGO.
You said you went to pay your respects, so I thought...
I... I DIDN'T KNOW.
About the Author
NO REASON WHY YOU WOULD KNOW. IT DIDN'T MAKE THE HEADLINE NEWS OR ANYTHING.
IN FACT, I'M MORE SURPRISED THAT YOU KNOW WHO HE IS.
WHAT A SMALL WORLD.
YEAH, HUH...
I went to pay my respects at his grave.
HMM...

I WONDER IF HE'D MIND ME ASKING MORE QUESTIONS?
Like how did they know each other?
HMM ...
HE DOESN'T SEEM TO HAVE A "DON'T ASK" LOOK.
BUT STILL...
OH, HEY...
FWP
WHOA!
OH! SORRY! YES?!
WHY WAS TERU IN A RUSH TO GO HOME? DOES SHE HAVE THE RUNS OR SOMETHING?
OH NO, NOTHING LIKE THAT. SHE'S LOOKING FOR HER BUS PASS.
WHAT? HER BUS PASS?
YEAH, SHE LOST IT YESTERDAY MORNING BEFORE SHE BOARDED THE BUS.
SHE WAS AWFULLY CURIOUS ABOUT THIS GUY AT THE BUS STOP.
SHE SAID THAT GUY LOOKED LIKE HER BROTHER ...
MAYBE SHE WASN'T PAYING ATTENTION AND DROPPED IT.
VROOO..

VROOOO...
HI THERE.
OH... IT'S HIM AGAIN...
SHUP
H-HELLO.
NICE TO SEE YOU AGAIN.
THAT'S AN INTERESTING POSITION. WHAT'RE YOU DOING?
HE'S TALKING TO ME...
OH! HA HA. HOW EMBARRASSING.
I'M ACTUALLY LOOKING FOR MY BUS PASS...
WHAT A NICE GUY...
SHA
YOU MEAN THIS?
!!!
That's ...!!
YES, YES! OH, THANK GOODNESS.
YOU FOUND IT? THANK YOU SO MUCH!
HEE HEE.
How lucky! I'm glad someone nice picked it up...

YOU WANT IT BACK?
THEN GIVE ME SOMETHING IN RETURN.
HUH?
YOU KNOW, AS A TOKEN OF YOUR APPRECIATION.
A SIMPLE "THANK YOU" JUST DOESN'T SEEM ENOUGH.
I-I GUESS YOU'RE RIGHT.
I'm the one who lost it.
RUMMAGE RUMMAGE
LET'S SEE... A CAN OF JUICE? OR SOME THANK-YOU MONEY...
The pass cost 2000 yen, so at most, 20 percent... which makes that 400 yen...
WHAT? IS THAT ALL?
FORGET IT.
I WANT SOMETHING MUCH BETTER.
SOMETHING YOU CAN'T BUY WITH MONEY.
FOR EXAMPLE...
WHAT...?
...LOVE.

NO WAY.
S...
WHAT *IS* THIS?

WHAT IS HE DOING?!
STOP IT...!
HUF
OW...
Why'd you hit me with your bag?
THAT WASN'T VERY NICE.
Y-YOU ASKED FOR IT! HOW DARE YOU?!
I CAN'T BELIEVE IT! I THOUGHT YOU WERE A NICE PERSON ...!
WHAT'S THE BIG DEAL? NO NEED TO GET SO UPSET.
HE'S HORRIBLE.
I WAS JUST TRYING TO BE FRIENDS. OKAY? *HEE HEE HEE.*
HEY, YOU'RE BLUSHING. WHAT'S THE MATTER?
HE'S...

DON'T TELL ME THAT WAS YOUR FIRST KISS?
...NOT LIKE SOICHIRO AT ALL.
DASH
HEY...
DON'T YOU WANT YOUR PASS BACK?
HEE HEE. OH WELL...
SEE YOU AGAIN, TERU.
NOT ON YOUR LIFE.

NOT EVER.
KISSED?
WHAT? WHO KISSED HER?
SOMEONE SHE DIDN'T KNOW WELL. I DIDN'T GET THE DETAILS ...
...BUT THIS GUY APPAR-ENTLY FOUND HER BUS PASS...
THAT DOESN'T EXPLAIN ANYTHING. WHY DIDN'T YOU GET MORE OUT OF HER?
I COULDN'T. SHE'S LOCKED HERSELF IN HER ROOM AND REFUSES TO EAT.
I'm surprised she told me even that much.
IT'S NOT LIKE HER TO ACT THIS WAY, SO SHE MUST BE QUITE UPSET.
ALSO... SHE DOESN'T WANT TO SEE YOU.

FWP
THAT'S FINE. TO BE HONEST, I DON'T FEEL LIKE SEEING HER NOW EITHER.
TELL HER, "QUIT MOPING AROUND BECAUSE OF SOME SILLY KISS."
WAIT, TASUKU! YOU'VE GOT IT ALL WRONG!
SHE'S FEELING TOO ASHAMED TO SEE YOU! YOU'RE NOT SO IMMATURE THAT YOU CAN'T SEE THAT, RIGHT?
WHAT SHE REALLY NEEDS IS TO HEAR YOU SAY EVERY-THING'S OKAY!
SHE DIDN'T DO ANYTHING WRONG...
I DON'T WANT TO SEE HER BECAUSE OF MY OWN REASONS.
SORRY, BUT I CAN'T SOOTHE HER FEELINGS RIGHT NOW.
OF COURSE NOT. I GET IT.
GIVE ME A BREAK, HUH? TRY TO UNDERSTAND HOW I FEEL.
IT WAS A SILLY KISS.
SO WHY...

...AM I SO RELUCTANT TO SEE HIM?
KNOCK KNOCK
TERU, I TOLD KUROSAKI WHAT HAPPENED.
HE SAID TO QUIT MOPING BECAUSE OF SOME SILLY KISS.
DEPRESSED
I-I SEE...
YOU CAN'T COUNT ON KUROSAKI. HE DOESN'T UNDER-STAND WOMEN.
YOU NEED TO TALK TO SOMEONE YOU REALLY TRUST.
WHY DO I FEEL SO DISAP-POINTED?
HEY, TERU...
AT LEAST I WASN'T ATTRACTED TO THAT GUY...
SWP
SOMEONE WHO'S KIND AND SINCERE ...
SOME-ONE WHO KNOWS JUST HOW TO COMFORT YOU WHEN YOU'RE HURTING ...

SOMEONE LIKE DAISY...
...THE MOST IMPORTANT PERSON IN YOUR LIFE, RIGHT?
DAISY, IT'S ME, TERU.
DOOT
SOMEONE I DON'T KNOW VERY WELL KISSED ME.
Daisy, it's me, Teru. Someone I don't know very well suddenly kissed me. It was such a shock. I don't know why, but I feel so depressed. I could really use some cheerful words from you right now. I was so hoping my first kiss would be with someone I love.
TAP
TAP TAP
TAP
...I FEEL SO DE-PRESSED.
Send message? Yes/No

I WAS SO HOPING MY FIRST KISS...
...WOULD BE WITH SOMEONE I LOVE.
TAP TAP TAP TAP TAP TAP TAP TAP TAP TAP TAP T TAP TAP TAP TAP TAP ...
DOOK
DEAR TERU...
I THINK YOU'RE MAKING IT INTO A MUCH BIGGER DEAL IN YOUR MIND THAN IT ACTUALLY IS.
THESE WORDS ARE SO LIKE DAISY TO SAY...
THIS DOESN'T CHANGE WHO YOU ARE AT ALL, SO DON'T GIVE IT ANOTHER THOUGHT.
YEAH, THAT'S ALL I NEEDED TO HEAR...
Dear Teru,
I'm sorry you were kissed by someone you don't even like. I can understand why an earnest girl like you would take it so hard. But this doesn't change who you are at all, so don't give it another thought. I think you're making it nto a much bigger deal your mind than it ually is. I'm certainly worried.
HUH?
nto a much bigger your mind than it actually is. I'm certain not worried.
Actually, I'm

ACTUALLY, I'M LYING. IT BOTHERS ME LIKE HELL.
I'D MAKE YOU FORGET THAT KID'S CLUMSY ATTEMPT AT KISSING...
IF I KNEW THIS WOULD HAPPEN, I WOULDN'T HAVE HELD BACK FOR SO LONG.
I WANT TO RUSH OVER THERE RIGHT NOW AND KISS YOU.
...IN AN INSTANT.

BEEP
JOLT
Pretend you never received that last message. It was a bad joke. Really. I'm sorry. Forgive me.
YOU'RE KIDDING...

WHAT THE HELL AM I DOING? I JUST CONFESSED...
I CAN'T BELIEVE I ACTUALLY SENT THAT...
THANK YOU, DAISY. YOUR WORDS MADE ME FORGET...
...WHAT WAS BOTHERING ME...
...INSTANTLY.
SOME-BODY KILL ME—!!
AAGHHH

THE NIGHT PASSED...
...AND MORNING CAME.
CHAK
MORNING, KUROSAKI.
YO.
I HEARD YOU HAD SOME TROUBLE LAST NIGHT.
CHAK CHAK
YUP, BUT I'M FINE NOW.
DAISY TOLD ME STUFF, LIKE HOW I SHOULDN'T WORRY.
WOBBLE
WELL, HE'S RIGHT. SO DON'T WORRY.
WOBBLE
STUMBLE
SHK SHK
IT WAS A REGULAR MORNING.

STILL, I'D LIKE TO FIND THE JERK WHO KISSED HER.
SOMEONE SHE DIDN'T KNOW WELL, HUH...
IF I EVER SEE HIM AGAIN, I'LL KICK HIS BUTT.
And he still has my pass...
OF ALL THE LUCK... SEEING SOMEONE LIKE THAT BY CHANCE, THREE TIMES IN A ROW...
HM, WAS IT A COINCIDENCE?
I'D BETTER BE CAREFUL.
HELLO.
ARE YOU PAYING A VISIT TO THE MIDORIKAWA GRAVE?
OH... YES. IT'S RIGHT UP AHEAD.

LAA
I KNOW.
TAKE CARE NOW.
A DAY THAT STARTS OUT PERFECTLY...
...CAN BE RUINED PRETTY EASILY...
JUST LIKE SOMEONE'S SILLY TOY...

リー

CHAPTER 32: A
LOST CHILD'S HEART

TASUKU...
HEY, TASUKU.
YOU'LL CATCH A COLD NAPPING OVER THERE.

AKIRA...

HE'S A CHARACTER THAT'S DIFFICULT TO FIGURE OUT. SORT OF CREEPY. I GUESS IT'S ALL RIGHT SINCE MY INTENTION IS TO DRAW AN UNREADABLE CHARACTER... I'M A LITTLE WORRIED ABOUT THE OUTCOME THOUGH.
I'M SORRY THIS MANGA HAS SO FEW GOOD-LOOKING MEN.
...BUT I DO SORT OF ENJOY DRAWING THIS CHARACTER... I WONDER WHY. IT'S STRANGE.

THANKS FOR WORKING SO LATE.
YOU FEELING RELIEVED AFTER FINISHING STAGE ONE?
CRAP... I MUST'VE DOZED OFF.
HEY, ABOUT THAT AFTERNOON DEADLINE...
I CHECKED YOUR WORK. IT'S ALL FIXED. YOU PASS.
WE'LL BE ABLE TO DELIVER ON TIME.
I KNOW I FORCED YOU TO BE THE TEAM LEADER, BUT YOU DID WELL.
I was hard on you, but you didn't break.
IT WAS PRETTY OBVIOUS YOU WERE UNDER A LOT OF STRESS, THOUGH.
YOU'VE DONE SOME PRETTY DANGEROUS STUFF AS A HACKER.
WORKING AN HONEST JOB WITH PEOPLE RELYING ON YOU WASN'T ANY EASIER, HUH?

THAT'S HOW YOU *SHOULD* BE FEELING.
Well done.
IT'S PROOF THAT YOUR HEART IS WHOLE AND HEALTHY.
I KNOW...
...THAT YOU REGRET THE THINGS YOU'VE DONE.
SO START CHERISHING THE THINGS YOU EXPERIENCE NOW.
THAT WAY, YOUR LIFE WON'T BE MADE OF PAST REGRETS.
ONE DAY, YOUR MEMORIES OF HARDSHIP WILL TURN INTO LIFE SKILLS...
...THAT'LL PROTECT YOU AND THOSE PRECIOUS TO YOU.
I HAVE NO DOUBT OF THAT.

WHAT'S WITH THE LECTURE? I DIDN'T GET ANY OF IT.
Hmph.
AND YOU CAN STOP WITH THE BIG BROTHER ACT.
SORRY, SORRY. THERE'S JUST SOMETHING ABOUT YOU THAT MAKES ME WANT TO CODDLE YOU.
I GET THE FEELING THAT SOMEWHERE DEEP DOWN INSIDE, YOU AND I ARE REALLY ALIKE.
WHOA, LOOK AT THE TIME.
I GOTTA GET OUT OF HERE. MY CUTE LITTLE SISTER'S WAITING.
Make yourself at home here.
OH YEAH... IT'S JUST YOU AND YOUR SISTER, HUH.
SHE PROBABLY WENT TO BED AGES AGO.
THAT'S OKAY. IN FACT, IT'S BETTER!
THEN I CAN GIVE HER SLEEPING FACE A KISS OR CUDDLE UP NEXT TO HER, RIGHT?
Hee hee. My little Teru...
If I tried that while she was awake, she'd get so mad.

WHAT A PERVERT. I FEEL SORRY FOR YOUR SISTER.
Gotta admit I've heard the rumors though.
SHE'S ADORABLE. SUCH AN ANGEL...
You just don't get it.
YOU'RE THE ONE I FEEL SORRY FOR, NOT KNOWING THE TRUTH.
IF YOU MET HER, YOU'D WANT TO DO THE SAME THING.
Which is why I won't introduce her to you.
I DON'T WANNA MEET HER OR DO THOSE THINGS.
I'M NOT A PERVERT, SO DON'T LUMP ME TOGETHER WITH YOU.
I WONDER ABOUT THAT.
DIDN'T I JUST SAY WE'RE ALIKE?
YOU'LL REALIZE THAT SOMEDAY.
HEH HEH HEH HEH HEH...

TWEET...
WHAT'S THE MATTER, TASUKU?
I DREAMED ABOUT SOICHIRO AGAIN LAST NIGHT...
Maybe he was right...
IT WAS THE WORST DREAM I'VE HAD LATELY.
ANYWAY, WHO DID YOU SEE ON YOUR WAY TO THE PROFES-SOR'S GRAVE?
SO YOU WERE LISTENING TO ME. HOW NICE.
If you don't mind a pervert like me, I'm all ears.
I DIDN'T KNOW THE GUY. WE JUST PASSED EACH OTHER.
HE REMINDED ME A LITTLE BIT OF SOICHIRO.
HIS OVERALL LOOKS, I MEAN...
HE SPOKE TO ME FIRST...
"HELLO. ARE YOU PAYING A VISIT TO THE MIDORIKAWA GRAVE?"
...SO I GOT A BETTER LOOK AT HIM.

WHAT? DID THEY LOOK THAT MUCH ALIKE?
NO. ACTUALLY, HE DIDN'T LOOK LIKE SOICHIRO AT ALL.
OKAY... SO WHAT'S THE BIG DEAL?
I KNOW, YOU'RE RIGHT. IT'S JUST...
THERE WAS SOMETHING ABOUT HIM THAT GAVE ME THE CREEPS.
HE EVEN MADE ME THINK THAT HE MIGHT BE...
...AKIRA.
HE WORE A HOODIE AND HAD BLACK HAIR. IT FITS.
I KNOW YOU CAN'T SINGLE OUT A PERSON BASED ON THOSE NOTES...
AKIRA
SORRY, I CAN'T DRAW. ARAI
*HEIGHT ABOUT 5'7"
*LONGISH BLACK HAIR
*HOODIE AND BASE
CAP - PUSHED DOW
LOW OVER HIS FACE
*TWISTED GRIN
*SLOUCHES
*RIDES A SCOOTE

...BUT WHAT IF HE'S THE SAME GUY...
...WHO KISSED TERU?
ZAA
I DON'T LIKE THIS FEELING.
I CAN'T TELL WHAT IT IS, BUT IT FEELS LIKE SOMETHING'S MOVING.
TAP
TAP TAP
I CAN SENSE IT...
Daisy, it's Te
I'm doing fi
today.

DO ONE GOOD DEED EACH DAY
OH, HELLO, KURO-SAKI.
It's horrendous. Did you catch a cold?
No, I'm fine.
DO GOOD EACH
WHAT'S WITH THAT MASK?
IT'S TO PREVENT ASSAULT ON A GIRL'S LIPS, 99% FOOLPROOF.
THIS IS THE PERFECT SELF-DEFENSE. NO ONE WOULD EVEN TRY TO KISS ME NOW!!
And it has a wise saying too!
TUG
DO ONE GOOD DEED EACH DAY
LOSE THIS. SERIOUS-LY.
IT DOESN'T LOOK GOOD AT ALL.
THEN HOW ABOUT THIS? STEEL WOOL.
SKRCH
AT FIRST GLANCE, IT'S JUST A MOUSTACHE. BUT TRY TO KISS ME, AND IT WILL *HURT*.
AND I CAN ALWAYS DO THE MOUS-TACHE DANCE.
DA DUM DA DUM DA DUM DA DUM
YAY!
I've seen that be-fore!
DA DUM DA DUM
AMAZING... I'VE NEVER SEEN THAT DONE LIVE.

HEY, COME ON!
ENOUGH OF YOUR SILLY ANTICS.
EVEN IF THAT OLD MAN OVER THERE IS NICE ENOUGH TO LAUGH...
It doesn't make the grade in my book.
CHIDE CHIDE
STILL, THAT DON'T-GIVE-IN ATTITUDE OF YOURS IS GOOD.
I'll praise you for that.
WELL, YEAH. AS IF I'D LET THAT JERK GET ME DOWN.
Oww...
I NEVER, EVER WANT SOMEONE TO KISS ME WITHOUT MY PERMISSION AGAIN.
I FEEL SO STUPID.
HE REMINDED ME OF MY BROTHER, SO I LET MY GUARD DOWN.
ESPECIALLY SINCE WE BUMPED INTO EACH OTHER THREE TIMES.
IT WAS WEIRD...
ZAA

I'M GETTING A BAD FEELING...
I'LL NEVER BE CARELESS AGAIN...
JUST LOSE THIS THING.
BUT THAT'S THE ONE WITHOUT THE SAYING.
YOU DON'T NEED IT NOW.
I'M RIGHT HERE.
STILL...
IF YOU'RE WORRIED, STAY CLOSE TO ME.

...WHEN I SEE YOUR SMILE...
...I FEEL SO RELIEVED.
WHY ARE YOU BEING SO NICE, KURO-SAKI?
DO YOU HAVE AN ULTERIOR MOTIVE?
WHATEVER HAPPENS...
I'M GOING TO SEE TAKEDA, AND YOU'RE COMING WITH ME. YOU'RE NOT ALLOWED TO REFUSE.
Seeing him by myself is torture.
...AS LONG AS SHE'S WITH ME, I CAN PROTECT HER.
Huh? Huh?
YAY! WILL I GET TO SEE KAORUKO TOO?
I'LL BE THE ONE STAYING CLOSEST TO HER.
THAT THOUGHT ALONE...

...MAKES ME WEAK AGAIN.

JUST WHEN I HAD DECIDED TO TELL HER THE WHOLE TRUTH...

DENGEKI DAISY
QUESTION CORNER
BALDLY ASK!!
Q.
•WHAT ARE SOME RECENT MANGA AND ANIME THAT KUROSAKI ENJOYS?
I BET IT'S ●●JI OR ●KAGI OR [EDITED].
•WHAT KIND OF VIDEO GAMES DOES HE RECOMMEND?
•WHERE DOES KUROSAKI GO ON HIS DAYS OFF?
(YUUYUU, MIYAZAKI PREFECTURE)
A.
• I'LL START WITH HIS DAYS OFF. HE'LL GO TO THE HARDWARE STORE FOR HIS DAILY ESSENTIALS. OR HE'LL STALK TERU, OR HE'LL GO TO THE BOOKSTORE, OR HE'LL GO TO BOSS'S PLACE, OR HE'LL STALK TERU, OR HE'LL GO WORK OUT AT THE GYM, OR HE'LL STALK TERU. VERY AVERAGE.
• GAMES HE'D RECOMMEND.. HMM... FF SERIES 7, 9, 10, AND TACTICS. THERE'S ALSO A GAME CALLED IQ (THEY'RE ALL ANCIENT GAMES). ACTUALLY, THE GAMES HE LIKES ARE THE ONES THE AUTHOR LIKES. MY APOLOGIES. MAN, I HAVEN'T PLAYED VIDEO GAMES IN AGES. I WISH I COULD PLAY RIGHT NOW. REALLY.
I THINK KUROSAKI WOULD LIKE WELL-KNOWN GAMES LIKE TETRIS AND THE ACE COMBAT SERIES (THE AIRCRAFT ONE). I ALSO THINK HE'D GET HOOKED ON MINESWEEPER, A GAME THAT'S IN THE WINDOWS ACCESSORIES FOLDER. I BET HE'D BE OBSESSED WITH IT HERE AND THERE.
• THIS AUTHOR HASN'T KEPT UP WITH RECENT ANIME AT ALL, SO I DON'T KNOW THEM. ...SORRY. BUT I THINK KUROSAKI WOULD LIKE KURENAI NO BUTA [PORCO ROSSO] FROM STUDIO GHIBLI. ...ALSO, KUROSAKI OFTEN READS A MANGA CALLED AKAHAGE THAT I THINK IS ABOUT MAHJONG. I'M NOT SURE, BUT THERE'S SUPPOSED TO BE A REAL MANGA LIKE IT. APPARENTLY WHEN YOU READ IT, IT MAKES YOU RESTLESS FOR SOME REASON... AND THAT'S ALL I HAVE TO SAY BEFORE THINGS GET RISKY!!!
I'LL LOOK INTO IT. ALONG WITH THIS "CHIHARU MORI."
DON'T GET YOUR HOPES UP THOUGH.
OKAY, THANKS.
SO?
THAT'S NOT ALL YOU WANTED TO SEE ME ABOUT, IS IT?
DON'T KEEP ME IN SUSPENSE. TELL ME.
WELL...
Okay, let's play fetch.

Go!
TAKEDA...
IF YOU WERE IN MY PLACE, WOULD YOU TELL TERU?
I MEAN EVERYTHING THAT I'VE KEPT FROM HER...
I FEEL LIKE SOMETHING BAD IS GOING TO HAPPEN...
...SO MAYBE I'D BETTER...
WHY ARE YOU ASKING ME SOMETHING SO SERIOUS?
We've never been chummy...
HA HA. YEAH, YOU'RE RIGHT.
I GUESS I FIGURED YOU'D BE BRUTALLY HONEST WITH ME.

IF YOU'RE ASKING ME...
...THEN YOU'RE *GOING* TO TELL HER.
Bring it to me...
No, no...
I GUESS.
① INSTEAD OF THE DOG, IT'S THE HUMAN DOING THE FETCHING.
No, Kaoruko...
Bring the ball to me.
② IT BECOMES A GAME OF TAG. (FETCH DIDN'T WORK.)
LUNGE
DASH
A WHILE AGO, I MADE UP MY MIND TO TELL HER...
...SO I DON'T WANT TO PUT IT OFF.
Wait, Kaoruko...
I WANT TO GET IT OVER WITH BEFORE I CHANGE MY MIND.
Hey! Wait up!

I KNOW I DECIDED TO TAKE ACTION.
I DO WANT TO GET IT OVER WITH.
BUT MAYBE IT'S JUST ME BEING SELFISH.
LIKE, "I'VE DECIDED. NO MORE WAVERING."
AM I TELLING MYSELF THAT JUST BECAUSE I'M TIRED OF THE BURDEN?
SHE'S THE ONE WHO'S GOING TO BE HURT WHEN SHE HEARS EVERYTHING.
Listen, you have to bring it back to me.
?
WELL, THAT'S...
BUT THEN...

...I REALIZE...
...I'M ACTUALLY SCARED TO TELL HER.
I'M FINDING EXCUSES BECAUSE I'M BEING A COWARD.
I DON'T KNOW WHAT TO THINK ANYMORE.
EVERY-THING SEEMS WRONG.
I START OUT TRYING TO DO THE RIGHT THING AND END UP THINKING ONLY ABOUT MYSELF.
JUST LIKE BACK THEN...
SOICHIRO...

TELL ME, SOICHIRO.
HOW DOES SOMEONE STAY TRUE TO HIMSELF?
THE WAY YOU ALWAYS WERE...
KUROSAKI...
KUROSAKI !!
OH
VSH
HUH...?

WHAM
I-I'M SO SORRY...
TMP
TMP
TMP
I THREW THE BALL REALLY HARD AND I HAVE BAD AIM...
NOOO! KUROSAKI!
What have I done?!
SHOCK
DON'T WORRY, HE'S FINE. HE'S JUST ACTING.
SHUUUUU
SNIFF
SNIFF
BESIDES, IT'S HIS FAULT FOR NOT DODGING IT.
It's a rubber ball. No big deal.
...
LICK LICK

Let's go out a little farther.
YOU'RE PRETTY SLOW, AREN'T YOU?
Got no one to blame but yourself.
NO, I'M NOT.
I JUST HAVE A TENDENCY TO GET LOST IN MY OWN THOUGHTS.
I know.
FSHH
SO YOU'RE CRAZY. I GET THAT.
HEH
YOU'RE THE TYPE THAT WORRIES ABOUT GETTING LOST, THEN TRIPS ON A PEBBLE RIGHT IN FRONT OF YOU.
Sorry, I'm always blunt.
YEAH, THAT'S FOR SURE. THANKS FOR BEING SO ENLIGHTENING, YOU JERK.
Damn, I'm out of cigarettes.
KRSH
ACTUALLY, I DO UNDERSTAND YOU.
WE'RE BOTH THE SAME TYPE OF FOOL.

I REALLY DO GET HOW YOU FEEL, BUT I'M NOT THE ONE WHO CAN HELP YOU.
SO FORGIVE ME.
Here, have one.
COFF
KIR
SADLY, YOU'RE NOT THE ONLY ONE...
...WHO FOCUSES SOLELY ON THE RISK AND CAN'T TAKE ACTION.
FUU
WE TELL OURSELVES THAT AT LEAST IT'S BETTER THAN THOSE WHO ARE TOTALLY HELPLESS.
BUT IN REALITY, THERE'S NOT MUCH DIFFER-ENCE.
IN BOTH CASES, DOING NOTHING DOESN'T WORK.
SO WE HAVE TO SWALLOW OUR PRIDE...
...AND LET SOMEONE TAKE US BY THE HAND...
...AND NOT COMPLAIN IF THE DESTINATION TURNS OUT TO BE HELL.

WORRYING ENDLESSLY IS A KIND OF HELL TOO.
AREN'T YOU SICK OF IT? BE HONEST.
You asked me for advice, so I'm telling you.
HA HA. YOU'RE RIGHT. I'M EXHAUSTED.
THEN SO WHAT IF THE DESTINATION TURNS OUT TO BE HELL?
AT LEAST YOU WON'T BE TIRED ANYMORE.
JUST LET THE GIRL YOU LOVE TAKE YOUR HAND...
...AND LEAD YOU TO WHATEVER HELL FOLLOWS.

I GUESS SO.
I COULDN'T HAVE ASKED...
...FOR BETTER ADVICE.
IT'LL BE MUCH BETTER...
...THAN BEING STUCK LIKE THIS.
GUESS WHAT, KUROSAKI!
HE JUST FETCHED! It was just once, but still!

TO BE HONEST...
Can you take our picture, Mr. Takeda?
Sure. Kurosaki, get in the picture too.
What? Forget it.
...I DO WISH...
...I WERE MORE LIKE YOU.
IF THAT WERE THE CASE...
Oh, come on, Kurosaki. Hurry up!
...I'D BE ABLE TO MAKE TERU HAPPY.
SOICHIRO...
IF I WERE LIKE YOU...

...NO MATTER HOW DIFFICULT THINGS GOT...
...I'D SET MY EYES ON PARADISE AND GET THERE WITHOUT GETTING LOST.
SIGH...
I'M STARVING.
FWP
FWP
WHERE'S THAT RAMEN PLACE?
I COULD'VE SWORN THERE WAS A SIGN AROUND HERE...
GURGLE
LET'S JUST GO EAT AT FLOWER GARDEN.
NO WAY! YOU'RE THE ONE WHO SAID YOU FELT LIKE EATING RAMEN IN THE FIRST PLACE!!
NOW I'M CRAVING RAMEN TOO! RAMEN!!
GRAAAH
You can't wait any longer, right?
Every-one gets these cravings like three times a year!

I WENT TO THIS RAMEN SHOP BEFORE WITH MY BROTHER.
WE MAY HAVE TO WAIT A LITTLE BIT MORE, BUT FOLLOW ME!
Their ramen is delicious!
HMM... WITH SOICHIRO, HUH?
Okay, sure.
Onward! Let's go!!
They serve kotteri ramen, so the soup is rich, and it's got lots of chopped green onions.
Kotteri ramen, huh?
THIS IS HARD...
HOW DO I BREAK IT TO HER?
HUH?
I WAS WRONG, AFTER ALL!!
DOOM
ADULT TOYS
NO ONE UNDER 18 PERMITTED INSIDE
SHOCK
SHOCK
SHOP
One thing's for sure—this isn't the place!
VWIP
HEY, DO YOU REALLY REMEMBER WHERE THIS PLACE IS?
I'm not into toys and stuff.
DON'T WORRY! I REMEMBER NOW. THIS WAY!!!

ACTUALLY, I JUST FOLLOWED SOICHIRO THAT TIME.
HE ALWAYS FINDS HIS WAY, SO I WASN'T...
...PAYING ATTEN-TION...
"HE ALWAYS FINDS HIS WAY"...
THAT'S FOR SURE.
HEH.
YOUR BROTHER MUST'VE BEEN PRETTY AMAZING.
I GUESS YOU'RE THE OPPOSITE OF HIM AND GET LOST QUITE OFTEN.
NO WAY, HE WASN'T AMAZING AT ALL.
HE HAD ABSO-LUTELY NO SENSE OF DIREC-TION.
I knew my way around much better than he did.
?
HE TRIED HARD NOT TO GET LOST...
...BUT HE ALWAYS MADE SOME MISTAKE.
Hmm...
That's strange ...
Soichiro ...
I'm hungry!
FOR ONE THING, HE COULDN'T READ MAPS.
HE NEVER MADE IT TO A DESTINATION WITHOUT MAKING A WRONG TURN FIRST. NOT ONCE.

HUH? DIDN'T YOU JUST SAY HE ALWAYS FINDS HIS WAY?
WELL, LET ME EXPLAIN.
HE NEVER GOT "LOST" LOST.
EVEN IF HE HAD TO BACKTRACK OR CHANGE ROUTES, HE ULTIMATELY MADE IT TO HIS DESTINATION.
HE ALWAYS SAID THIS...
"AS LONG AS YOU DON'T GIVE UP, YOU'RE NEVER LOST.
"IF YOU END UP SOMEWHERE YOU DON'T WANT TO BE...
"...JUST FIND A CONNECTING ROUTE.
"THEN YOU'RE SURE TO REACH YOUR ULTIMATE DESTINATION."

IF YOU THINK HARD...
...MAKE A CHOICE, AND START WALKING...
...THAT ROAD IS SURE TO TAKE YOU WHERE YOU WANT TO GO.
MY GOD...
...SOICHIRO...
HA HA...
ARE YOU SERIOUS?
Yes! It's true!
AH HA HA HA HA
RIDICULOUS, ISN'T IT? THE THINGS HE SAID...
ISN'T THAT THE RATIONALE OF A TOTALLY DIRECTION-CHALLENGED PERSON?
SERIOUSLY...
WHO WERE YOU?
I'm so glad you think it's funny too.
Ah ha ha...
I USED TO LAUGH SO HARD...

...UNTIL I BEGAN TO THINK I'M JUST LIKE HIM.
WHAT KIND OF PERSON WERE YOU?
KUROSAKI, YOU DON'T HAVE TO LAUGH THAT MUCH!
BUT IT IS A NEAT WAY OF THINKING, HUH?
HOW ...?
Eh heh heh
IT PUTS YOUR MIND AT EASE.
HOW DID YOU KNOW...
...THOSE WERE THE WORDS I WANTED TO HEAR AT THIS VERY MOMENT?
RIGHT? IT'S NOT A BAD WAY OF THINKING.
SO LET'S GO FIND THIS PLACE USING MY BROTHER'S METHOD.
We'll take it nice and slow.

"JUST...
COME ON, LET'S GO.
"...LET THE GIRL YOU LOVE TAKE YOUR HAND...
I'LL TAKE YOU.
"... AND LEAD YOU..."

KURO-SAKI...?
WHAT'S WRONG, KUROSAKI ...?
I'LL START WALKING.
LISTEN, TERU... NEXT SUNDAY...
LET'S YOU AND I GO SOME-WHERE.

WE'LL GO WHEREVER YOU LIKE. JUST THE TWO OF US.
THERE'S SOME-THING I WANT TO TELL YOU.
SOMETHING VERY IMPORTANT.
AND EVEN IF IT LEADS TO HELL...
...I'LL KEEP BELIEVING THAT IT'S A ROAD...
...WHERE HOPE GROWS.

THE BEST ☆ OF ☆ THE SECRET SCHOOL CUSTODIAN OFFICE ♥
LET'S GO STRAIGHT INTO THE SECOND ONE!
THERE IS A DENGEKI DAISY FAN SEGMENT BOLDLY FEATURED IN BETSUCOMI THAT IS APTLY TITLED "THE SECRET SCHOOL CUSTODIAN OFFICE ♥"! WITH DISCRIMINATING EYES, WE EXAMINED ALL THE GREAT WORK FEATURED THERE AND PICKED THE "BEST" AMONG THEM THAT WE WANTED TO LEAVE FOR POSTERITY!
THE "BEST OF" FOR VOLUME 7... IS THE "DAISY 'KANJI' PICKS"!
OUR THEME WAS "THIS YEAR'S KANJI," AND WE ASKED READERS TO USE A WORD IN KANJI TO BEST DESCRIBE EACH CHARACTER. NATURALLY, THE KANJI FOR "BALD" WAS OFF-LIMITS, BUT WE RECEIVED SOME WONDERFUL, GRADE A ENTRIES NONETHELESS!
DAISY "KANJI" PICKS!
GOOD WORDS THAT EMBODY THE PERSONALITIES OF EACH CHARACTER!
TASUKU KUROSAKI
→TERU, SINCE WITHOUT HER, KUROSAKI COULDN'T EXIST.☆
-CHOBI, IWATE PREFECTURE
照
TERU
WHAT'S WRONG WITH GETTING WORKED UP ABOUT HER?
●HE PROTECTS TERU WHILE STAYING IN THE BACKGROUND, SO SHU (守) FOR "PROTECT." ● KAN (漢) AS IN "MAN," I BELIEVE. ● THE THINGS KUROSAKI SAYS ALWAYS MAKES ME LAUGH, SO SHO (笑) FOR "LAUGH." ● I THINK THE FEELINGS HE HAS FOR TERU IS LOVE, SO AI (愛)... PLUS MANY MORE.
TERU KUREBAYASHI
→SHE IS THE PICTURE OF HEALTH, AND BEING A YOUNG GIRL IN LOVE, SHE IS HAPPY AND CHEERFUL. HENCE, KEN (健) [FOR "HEALTH"].
-HONEY, AICHI PREFECTURE
健
KEN
GOT AN AUTOGRAPH
BOING
●AFTER DISCOVERING THAT KUROSAKI IS DAISY, HER FEELINGS FOR HIM DEEPENED, SO KOI (恋) FOR "LOVE." ●SHE IS TRUE TO HERSELF ALL THE TIME, SO SEI (清) FOR "PURE," PLUS MANY MORE.
MASUDA (BOSS)
薇
ZENMAI
-JUENOE, MIE PREFECTURE
I'M SORRY ABOUT EVERY-THING...
↑AS A ZENMAI, OR FERN, HE WOULDN'T STAND OUT. BUT COMBINED WITH HIS PARTNER (KUROSAKI = GRASS), THEY BLOSSOM INTO A BRIGHT EXISTENCE.
KAZUMASA ANDO
受
UKERU
REALLY?
-DEREDERE DAIMAOU, GIFU PREFECTURE
↑THE ULTRA-MASOCHISTIC DIRECTOR ALWAYS SEEMS TO BE ON THE "RECEIVING END" OF THINGS, SO UKERU FOR "RECEIVE."
THANK YOU FOR ALL YOUR ENTRIES! ♡
I had no entries?
JUDGE'S COM-MENTS
IT WAS IRRITATING TO SEE "BOING" AS A TYPESET HERE.
(HEAD JUDGE: KYOUSUKE MOTOMI)
I DON'T THINK COMMENTS LIKE THAT ARE RELEVANT IN THESE INSTANCES!
(JUDGE: EDITOR FOR DENGEKI DAISY)
BETSUCOMI, THE MAGAZINE THAT SERIALIZES DAISY, GOES ON SALE EVERY MONTH AROUND THE 13TH! PLEASE LOOK FOR IT IF YOU WANT TO READ "THE SECRET SCHOOL CUSTODIAN OFFICE"! ♥

CHAPTER 33: I'LL BE ABLE TO SEE YOU

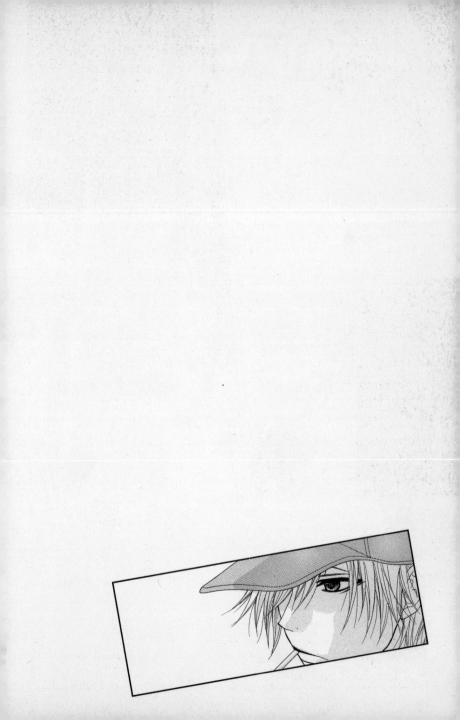

WAS I BEING NAIVE THIS WHOLE TIME?
I THOUGHT WE WERE FRIENDS.
WELL, NO MORE.
GO WHEREVER YOU WANT.
YOU TRAITOR.
I NEVER EXPECTED THIS.
I'M GLAD EVERYONE LIKES KAORUKO (THE DOG). I THINK I KNOW THE REASON. I PUT THREE TIMES (?) MORE EFFORT INTO DRAWING IT THAN I DO WITH DRAWING KUROSAKI.
AT THE SAME TIME, TAKEDA (WITH THE SALARY MAN GLASSES) SEEMS TO BE GROWING IN POPULARITY. I WONDER WHY. I MEAN, THIS MANGA DOESN'T HAVE GOOD-LOOKING MEN, SO MAYBE THAT'S HOW THIS HAPPENS?
HE'S BEEN HARD TO DRAW LATELY (I'VE NEVER BEEN ABLE TO CASUALLY DRAW HIM ANYWAY). WHAT'S WITH YOUR HAIRSTYLE?! DO YOU WANT IT ALL PUSHED BACK OR PARTED IN THE CENTER? MAKE UP YOUR MIND, TAKEDA!! DON'T GET CARRIED AWAY, TAKEDA!! AND GO POLISH YOUR GLASSES!!!!
I enjoy drawing Kaoruko, but he takes so long to draw. That's why I can't put him in the story too often.
GNAW GNAW♡

NO, I GUESS I DID.
FINE. SO WHAT SHOULD I PICK?
Let's see...
RECOMMENDED! THE TOP 100 BEST DATE SPOTS
THE TOP 100 BEST DATE SPOTS
WHAT DO YOU RECOMMEND, RENA?
HOLD IT! DON'T TELL ME YOU'RE ACTUALLY GOING?!
SHOCK
THE LEAST YOU CAN DO IS HAVE SOME RESPECT!
"NEXT SUNDAY... LET'S YOU AND I GO SOMEWHERE.
"WE'LL GO WHEREVER YOU LIKE..."
KUROSAKI SAID THAT TO ME YESTERDAY...
IN OTHER WORDS, IT'S A DATE, YOU IDIOT!
WELL, CONGRATULATIONS.
JUST LEAVE ME AND FIND HAPPINESS, DAMN IT.
WHACK
IT'S NOTHING LIKE THAT...
HE SAID HE HAS SOMETHING IMPORTANT TO SAY.
OH, BE QUIET. THAT JUST SOUNDS LIKE A PRELUDE TO HAPPINESS.
You know...
I wonder why Haruka can't find a boyfriend...
That's what I'd like to know.
GRRR

Heh.
WHAT OTHER *IMPORTANT THING* DO YOU HAVE TO SAY AFTER A DATE? IT HAS TO BE A CONFESSION OF LOVE.
Lucky for you, huh?
HE'LL SAY, "IN CASE YOU HAVEN'T NOTICED, I HAVE A LOLITA COMPLEX. SO GO OUT WITH ME."
YOU'RE WRONG.
IT WON'T BE ANYTHING LIKE THAT.
I'M PRETTY DENSE, BUT EVEN I CAN TELL.
I CONFIDED IN YOU TWO BEFORE, DIDN'T I?
KUROSAKI IS DAISY.
AND THAT'S NOT THE ONLY THING. HE HAS AN IMPORTANT SECRET THAT'S BEEN TROUBLING HIM.
DAISY SAID THAT HE'LL TELL ME HIS SECRET WHEN HE'S ABLE TO REVEAL HIS TRUE IDENTITY.

I HAVE A FEELING THAT TIME HAS COME.
I'M SORRY. I FEEL KIND OF NERVOUS.
I TOLD MYSELF THAT NO MATTER HOW SHOCKING THE NEWS WILL BE, I'LL LISTEN CALMLY.
BUT I DON'T KNOW HOW I'LL RESPOND TO HIS WORDS.
I DON'T KNOW HOW HE EXPECTS ME TO REACT.
I DON'T EVEN KNOW IF I'LL BE SYMPATHETIC.
WHAT IF KUROSAKI BECOMES DISAPPOINTED IN ME...?
SHA

SHUT UP!!
THWAK
SHE JUST TOOK YOU DOWN WITH A FINGER. TALK ABOUT BRUTE STRENGTH...
Is this the real you?
SHUULUUU...
AS A WOMAN, I FIND YOUR TRAIN OF THOUGHT UNFORGIV-ABLE.
FUU
YOU'RE GOING TO PRE-PLAN YOUR REACTION TO SUIT HIS EXPECTA-TIONS?
THAT'S MEANING-LESS AND PLAIN DISHONEST.
It's something a woman does only to stop her man from leaving her.
YOU'LL ONLY GET HURT. TAKE IT FROM A WOMAN WHO'S BEEN THERE BEFORE.
HUH...?
I LAUGHED THINGS OFF AND FORGAVE MY BOYFRIEND WHEN HE STOLE MONEY FROM MY WALLET. HE EVEN HIT ME BEFORE.
Of course I was angry, but I didn't want to lose him.
THEN HE'D SAY, "DON'T YOU WANT TO REHABILITATE ME?"
Really...?
Your experience with men sucks...
WHAT I'M SAYING IS, IT'S USELESS TO FRET ABOUT THESE THINGS.
If a relationship is meant to fail, it will. It doesn't matter what you say.
OH... I SEE...

THIS MAY SOUND TRITE...
...BUT YOU SHOULD LISTEN TO HIM WITH AN OPEN MIND...
...AND THEN ANSWER HIM HONESTLY.
IT MAY NOT ALWAYS WORK.
BUT I THINK THIS TIME, IT'S THE RIGHT THING TO DO.
SHE'S RIGHT. DON'T WORRY.
You'll manage some-how.
BESIDES, THERE'S NOTHING MORE IMPORTANT IN THIS WORLD THAN A DATE.
There, there.
SO FIRST AND FOREMOST, HAVE A GREAT TIME.
YOU TWO CAN TALK AFTER THAT.

YOU'RE REALLY LOOKING FORWARD TO THIS, RIGHT?
YES, I AM.
I'll go with you to get new panties.
Why new panties?
Oh, new panties are a must.
I MEAN...
AFTER ALL...
...THIS'LL BE MY VERY FIRST DATE WITH KUROSAKI.

IT'S GOING TO BE SO MUCH FUN.
HOW CAN IT NOT BE?
HMM... THE AMUSEMENT PARK, HUH?
IS THAT OKAY?
AMUSEMENT PARK
SPECIAL EVENT
EXCITING ZOOS
OR MAYBE NOT?
IT'S FINE WITH ME.
IT'S NEARBY AND SO CLICHÉ. ARE YOU BEING THOUGHTFUL?
SERIOUSLY, CHOOSE WHATEVER YOU WANT TO DO.
REALLY? WELL, THEN...

MY OTHER CHOICES ARE PANNING FOR GOLD OR PAINTING KOKESHI DOLLS...
...OR MAYBE GOING TO A TEMPLE FOR MEDITATION ...
AN ENCOUNTER WITH GOLD DUST
KOKESHI
CHANGE THAT BAD ATTITUDE
STRICT
TRAINING AT A TEMPLE
But my friends dis-couraged me from these options.
WHUP
LET'S GO TO THE AMUSEMENT PARK, AFTER ALL.
We can do those high-brow things another time.
I LOVE AMUSE-MENT PARKS.
Why?! You said it's my choice.
But painting kokeshi dolls... That sounds hard...
I WONDER WHY...
Actually, you look like a kokeshi... Both your face and body shape.
How dare you! I hope you lose your hair, Kurosaki!
ACTUALLY...
Fine, but I get to choose all the rides, no questions asked.
Even the Teacup. Okay?
Yeah, sure.
...I FEEL JUST FINE.
Those Teacup rides are scream-inducing though.
SHUP...
PUT THIS AROUND YOUR NECK.
IT'S PRETTY COLD TODAY.

MAKE SURE YOU KEEP WARM.
IF YOU CATCH A COLD, WE WON'T BE ABLE TO GO.
HEY, KUROSAKI...
I'M REALLY LOOKING FORWARD TO IT.

HEH HEH... YOUR SCARF HAS AN OLD—
...CIGARETTE SMELL.
YOU WERE ABOUT TO SAY "OLD MAN SMELL," HUH?
IT'S GOING TO BE SUCH A FUN DAY.
SNACKS WESTERN FOOD
* FLOWER GARDEN
I HEARD ABOUT IT TOO. EVEN ANDO KNOWS.
FHUU
TASUKU CAME OVER YESTERDAY AND TOLD US.
HE'S GOING TO TAKE TERU OUT AND TELL HER EVERYTHING. IT'S NEXT SUNDAY, RIGHT?
HE JUST SEEMED SO *CALM* ABOUT IT.

RIKO, YOU'RE WORRYING TOO MUCH.
DON'T LOOK LIKE THAT.
THINK ABOUT WHY WE NEVER...
...WANTED TO BREAK OUR TIES WITH TASUKU.
Have some coffee.
IT WASN'T SIMPLY BECAUSE SOICHIRO ASKED US NOT TO.
I HAVE FAITH THAT TERU WILL UNDER-STAND.
EVEN IF IT ENDS UP TAKING SOME TIME...
I KNOW THAT YOU WANT THEM BOTH TO BE HAPPY.
THAT'S WHY YOU'RE WORRIED.
BUT NOW IS WHEN YOU HAVE TO SIMPLY STAND BY THEM.

...
YOU'RE RIGHT...
IT'LL BE FINE.
I KNOW I'LL BE OKAY...
...NO MATTER WHAT YOU TELL ME.
Daisy, it's me, Teru. I'm doing great. Thank you for always looking out for me. Something exciting is going to happen next Sunday, and I can hardly wait.
IT'S BECAUSE I KNOW THE KIND OF PERSON YOU ARE.
SO YOU'RE GOING TO THE AMUSEMENT PARK?
YES! DO YOU KNOW WHICH RIDES ARE FUN THERE?
I went there just recently.

GO TO THEIR WEBSITE. IT HAS LOTS OF INFORMATION.
GOOD IDEA! I CAN GO ONLINE IN THE COMPUTER ROOM.
BOYS' LOCKER ROOM
HEY, KIYOSHI!
ISN'T THIS YOUR CELL PHONE?
I FOUND IT ON THE GROUND BEHIND THE GYM.
Did you lose it?
Oh!
I DID, THANKS!
I WAS JUST LOOKING FOR IT...
BEHIND THE GYM? HOW...?
I DIDN'T GO THERE. THERE'S NO WAY I COULD'VE DROPPED IT...
COMPUTER ROOM
YOU NEED TO TYPE IN YOUR USER ID...
TAP TAP ...
GO TO "SEARCH"... THEN TYPE IN "AMUSEMENT PARK"...

DENGEKI DAISY QUESTION CORNER

BALDLY ASK!!

Q.
IN VOLUME 6, KUROSAKI GAVE TERU MOUTH-TO-MOUTH RESUSCITATION. TERU WAS DEFINITELY NOT OBLIVIOUS TO IT, BUT WHAT ABOUT KUROSAKI? IF HE SAID SOMETHING LIKE, "HUH? THAT DIDN'T MEAN [OMITTED]," I'M GOING TO TEAR UP THE COMIC. ✦ ... THAT IS, I MIGHT. ♡

(SHIROGANE, HYOGO PREFECTURE)

A.
OH, I WOULDN'T BLAME YOU FOR GETTING MAD IF HE SAID THAT. BUT PROBABLY, IN THAT SITUATION, KUROSAKI DIDN'T EVEN THINK ABOUT IT LIKE THAT. SO IT CAN'T BE HELPED IF YOU TEAR THE COMIC TO SHREDS. I'M SORRY. (IF POSSIBLE, PLEASE PURCHASE ANOTHER COPY. ♡) AT TIMES LIKE THAT, YOU'RE DESPERATE TO SAVE A LIFE. NATURALLY, HE ACTED OUT OF LOVE. BUT A KISS AND MOUTH-TO-MOUTH RESUSCITATION ARE TWO DIFFERENT THINGS. (SORRY IF I DESTROYED YOUR DREAM). SO SOMEDAY, IF KUROSAKI IS DROWNING AND BOSS GIVES HIM MOUTH-TO-MOUTH RESUSCITATION... PLEASE... FORGIVE HIM.

Q.
WHEN KUROSAKI IS BEING AFFECTIONATE WITH TERU, DOES HE GET A NOSEBLEED?

(M.Y., HOKKAIDO)

A.
I DON'T THINK SO. WHEN KUROSAKI IS BEING AFFECTIONATE WITH HER, I THINK HE DOES IT SUBCONSCIOUSLY. HE'D PROBABLY (?) SAY, "MY BODY JUST REACTED THAT WAY." IN FACT, WHEN HE'S ALONE, HE PROBABLY IMAGINES THINGS THAT GIVE HIM NOSEBLEEDS OR SOMETHING ELSE. SORRY TO BE SO UNCOUTH. BUT YOU KNOW, THAT'S PROBABLY HOW MEN ARE.

COME BACK, AKIRA.
WE NEED TO GET READY TO GO OUT.
...YES, THE AMUSEMENT PARK.
WRR...
NOW BE A GOOD BOY AND DO AS I SAY...
AOZORA AMUS
GUIDE
POOL
TICKETS
PARKING
GROUP INFO
DOOT
DOOT DOOT DOOT
Daisy, it's Teru. Tomorrow is the big day!
TERU, ABOUT TOMORROW...
OH, YEAH! I'M LEAVING IN THE MORNING TO GO TO THE AMUSEMENT PARK!
RIGHT. WELL, HAVE FUN.
CALL ME IF ANYTHING COMES UP.
HEH HEH. I'LL BE FINE!
But I will!

RIGHT NOW AND FOREVER-MORE...
...YOU ARE THE MOST PRECIOUS PERSON IN MY LIFE.
DAISY...
I FINALLY...
...GET TO MEET YOU...

HEY, HEY, HEY! WHAT'S THE MATTER, HUH?
QUIT SQUEAL-ING OVER SOME-THING THIS TAME.
I... I'VE NEVER RIDDEN ANY-THING LIKE THIS BEFORE!
KURO-SAKI, DO THAT SOME MORE!
AH HA HA HA HA HA HA HA HA HA HA HA HA HA!!
WRRL
WOOOOOAA
WHEE! THIS IS SOOOO AWE-SOME!
WRRL
WRRL
WRRL
NO!
Daddy, do that too.

THE TEACUP WAS SO MUCH FUN.
I DIDN'T KNOW YOU'RE SUPPOSED TO MAKE IT SPIN LIKE THAT.
ACTUALLY, YOU'RE NOT.
FWSH
HA HA.
You're all flushed.
There.
YOUR HAIR'S A MESS.
WHAT DO YOU WANT TO RIDE NEXT?
HM, LET'S SEE...
OH! THAT ONE!
IF YOU CAN'T GET PAST THEM, YOU CAN'T GET OUT!
HAUNTED HOUSE
WARNING
OH... YOU DON'T WANT TO?
Are you scared?
I don't have veto rights any-way.
STUPID! IT'S FINE WITH ME. I'M NOT SCARED.
I'M NOT SCARED, STUPID.
Second time
C'MON, LET'S GO.

DON'T LET GO OF MY HAND. GOT THAT?
ANSWER ME!!
GRAAH
DO *NOT* LET GO OF MY HAND. I MEAN IT!!
If you let go, I'm gonna cry..
Oh, you're such a scaredy cat.
UH, OKAY.
LAND
DOESN'T CARE ANYMORE
SHOOTING GAME

ROLLER COASTER
HURRICANE
ARE YOU HAVING FUN, TERU?
HUH? OF COURSE I AM.
I'M HAVING TONS OF FUN. WHY?
GOOD.
I'M GLAD.
IT'S STILL EARLY AND I DON'T WANT TO RUSH THINGS...
...SO LET'S RIDE THE FERRIS WHEEL LAST.
FOR TWO?
YOU CAN PUT YOUR BELONGINGS HERE.
Oh, okay.
Next, please.
Just one.
Please place your things here...

This one's scary too. Don't wet yourself now.
If you get scared, I'll hold your hand.
You should talk.
You're the one who was scared earlier.
THIS IS SO MUCH FUN, KUROSAKI.
REALLY...
...REALLY FUN.
THEY DON'T SELL COLA HERE.
THEY HAVE SOME VENDING MACHINES NEAR THE SHOOTING GAME, SO I'LL GET THEM THERE.
OH, TOO BAD.
2nd. BALLOON
MENU

THAT'S OKAY, KURO-SAKI. IT DOESN'T HAVE TO BE COLA...
DON'T BE ABSURD. ONLY COLA GOES WITH PIZZA! NOTHING ELSE.
JUST WAIT HERE. I'LL BE RIGHT BACK.
USUALLY, HE SENDS ME TO GO GET THINGS...
THIS IS SO GREAT. I LOVE HOW HE'S TREATING ME SO NICE.
I'll wait for him right here.
MAYBE I'LL SEND RIKO A MESSAGE, ALONG WITH THAT...
...MERRY-GO-ROUND PIC I TOOK...
WHAT...?
THIS...
...ISN'T MY CELL PHONE.

W-WHY...? WHOSE IS THIS?

AND WHEN...?

CHAK...

WHAT HAPPENED TO MY CELL PHONE?!

Signal 1:52

Hi Teru.
I have your cell phone.
I'm waiting in front of the Ferris Wheel.
Please hurry.
Come alone.
Akira

GZZZZ-R

RINNNG...
HUH? SOME-ONE'S CALLING ME...
Teru...?
RINNNG...
Incoming Call
Unknown Caller
WHO IS THIS?
...
HELLO, KUROSAKI. IT'S BEEN A LONG TIME.
CAN YOU GUESS WHO I AM?
YOU DON'T KNOW? HOW RUDE.
YOU THOUGHT I WAS PRETTY AND CAME ON TO ME.
REMEM-BER? IN THE INFIRMARY...?
HEH HEH...
uca
COFFEE

YOU'VE GOT SOME NERVE CALLING ME...
...CHIHARU MORI.
HOW'D YOU GET MY NUMBER ...?!
SOME PEOPLE DON'T TRUST YOU NEARLY AS MUCH AS YOU THINK.
REALLY.
SOMEONE TOLD ME.
SOMEONE WHO YOU THOUGHT WAS A FRIEND.
I'LL PROVE IT TO YOU BY TELLING YOU SOMETHING.

YOUR DEAR LITTLE TERU...
...IS RIDING ON THE FERRIS WHEEL WITH SOMEONE ELSE RIGHT NOW.
WRR...
HMM...
WRR...
THIS IS PRETTY BORING.
IT'S SLOW AND DOESN'T GO THAT HIGH.
WRR...
SO GIRLS LIKE THIS SORT OF THING, HUH?
YOU TOO?
WRR...
ENOUGH ALREADY.

GIVE ME BACK MY CELL PHONE.
PLEASE, JUST GIVE IT BACK!!
AW, COME ON.
I'LL RETURN IT WHEN THIS RIDE STOPS.
Why don't you come and sit next to me?
IT'LL STOP SOON. IN THE MEANTIME, WE CAN CHAT...
Over my dead body! I still haven't forgiven you for that kiss!
WHAT? YOU TOLD ME YOU'D RETURN MY PHONE ONCE WE GOT ON THE FERRIS WHEEL!!
SO YOU'RE AKIRA, HUH?
IF I'D KNOWN EARLIER, I WOULDN'T HAVE GIVEN YOU THE TIME OF DAY.
WHAT'S YOUR CONNECTION TO MS. MORI?
WHY DID YOU WANT MY CELL PHONE SO BADLY...?!
HEY, NOW. DON'T ASK ME COMPLICATED QUESTIONS.

I'LL LET YOU GO ONCE THE RIDE STOPS...
I DON'T BELIEVE YOU!!
LUNGE
I'M SICK OF TALKING TO YOU! AND THIS FERRIS WHEEL DOESN'T STOP!
IT JUST KEEPS GOING ON AND ON... EVEN IF WE GET TO THE BOTTOM, IT JUST...
HEE HEE. I KNOW.
BUT IT'S GOING TO STOP ***TODAY***.
JUST FOR YOU.

BA-BUMP
HUH?
It stopped...
AAAAH!
Please pardon the inconvenience...
BEEP BEEP

I'm sorry, we're...
What happened?
WHY DID THE FERRIS WHEEL STOP? IS IT BROKEN?!
RAGH
PLEASE CALM DOWN. WE'RE CHECKING IT OUT RIGHT NOW.
RAGH
TELL ME WHAT'S GOING ON!
RAGH
WHAT ABOUT THE PEOPLE ON THE RIDE?
BEEP BEEP BEEP
THERE ARE CHILDREN ON IT!!
WAAH!
Please stand back.
What's going on?
WE'RE ASSESSING WHAT NEEDS TO BE DONE AND WILL MAKE IMMEDIATE REPAIRS...
AAAH!
LET THE PEOPLE IN THE LOWER CARS GET OFF!
What happened?
It came to a sudden stop just now.
Are there people on it?
IS THIS REALLY JUST ANOTHER BREAKDOWN? EARLIER...
WHAT IS THIS? DID YOU CAUSE IT?
WHAT DO YOU THINK?
Heh heh...
WHAT HAPPENS NEXT IS ALL UP TO YOU.

YOU'LL FIND OUT WHAT DAISY MUST DO...
...FROM TERU.
WHAT?! WHAT HAVE YOU DONE WITH TERU?
BEEP...
!!
Message Received
Teru_K

DAISY...
I BELIEVED YOU.
THAT TODAY WOULD BE A FUN DAY...
DON'T LOOK LIKE THAT, TERU.
BECAUSE I'D BE SEEING YOU...
ARE YOU IN SHOCK?
I FEEL BAD FOR YOU, BUT IN THIS CASE...

...YOU ONLY HAVE YOURSELF TO BLAME FOR BEING FOOLED.

I NEVER DREAMED...

om: Teru_K
Subject:
14:38

Daisy
I can't forgive you for killing my brother.
Please just disappear from my life.

...THAT THINGS WOULD END UP...

...LIKE THIS.

CHAPTER 34: TRUTH REARS ITS HEAD

"LET'S RIDE THE FERRIS WHEEL LAST."
THAT'S WHAT YOU SAID.

SINCE SHE IS SIMILAR TO A REAL VILLAINESS CHARACTER, I WANTED HER TO BE LIKE DORO● JO AND MAKE BOLD ENTRANCES, GET BEATEN BADLY, AND HAVE HER BOOBS SLIP OUT ONCE IN A WHILE. BUT IT'S DIFFICULT TO PLAY THAT ROLE IF HER BOOBS AREN'T DOING THEIR JOB.

AT SOME POINT IN THE NEAR FUTURE, I'M THINKING OF ASKING MY BEST FRIEND AND FELLOW MANGAKA MIKU MOMONO SENSEI (CURRENTLY HOT IN *BETSUCOMI* AND MOBAFLA), WHO IS A GENIUS AT DRAWING BOOBS, TO GIVE ME SOME INTENSE LESSONS SO THAT I CAN GET TRAINING.

SORRY TO KEEP GOING ON AND ON ABOUT BOOBS.

CHIHARU MORI

FROM THE TIME SHE DEBUTED IN THE STORY, I'VE DRAWN HER AS SOMEONE PULLING THE STRINGS BEHIND THE SCENES. AND WHEN HER TRUE IDENTITY WAS EXPOSED, SHE'D MAKE A BIG SPLASH AS A REAL VILLAINESS. AND THAT'S FINE. BUT FOR SOME REASON, I CAN'T DRAW HER BOOBS THAT WELL AFTER HER IDENTITY WAS REVEALED.

I GUESS I'M NOT GOOD AT DRAWING BOOBS.

ONCE WE WERE ALONE IN THAT SMALL SPACE...
...YOU WERE GOING TO TELL ME THAT YOU'RE DAISY...
...AND SHARE THE PAINFUL SECRET THAT YOU'VE KEPT TO YOURSELF FOR SO LONG.
THAT'S WHAT YOU WERE PLANNING TO DO, RIGHT?
I THOUGHT IT WOULD BE THE PERFECT PLACE...
...WHERE I COULD QUIETLY LISTEN TO YOUR STORY.
AND YET...

OUR SINCERE APOLOGIES TO ALL RIDERS.
WE ARE INVESTIGATING THE CAUSE AND WILL MAKE IMMEDIATE REPAIRS.
WAAH WAAH
I'm scared, Daddy!
HURRY UP AND GET US DOWN!
THIS THING BETTER NOT COLLAPSE.
You're kidding me! Nooo...
QUIT SHAKING THIS THING, YOU IDIOT! IT'S DANGEROUS!
THE FERRIS WHEEL HAS STOPPED DUE TO A MALFUNCTION...
PLEASE DO NOT ENDANGER YOURSELF OR OTHERS. STAY CALM AND REMAIN SEATED.
HEY, WE HAVE A SICK WOMAN HERE! DO SOMETHING!!
MOTHER, ARE YOU ALL RIGHT?!
KOFF KOFF
I REPEAT. THE FERRIS WHEEL HAS STOPPED DUE TO A MALFUNCTION...

SORRY FOR UPSETTING YOU, TERU...
...BUT YOU REALLY SHOULD TALK TO ME.
I MEAN, YOU GOT ALL THE PEOPLE ON THE FERRIS WHEEL INVOLVED NOW.
B'BMP
CHIHARU THINKS NOTHING OF DOING THIS KIND OF THING.
THEY'RE CRAZY.
B'BMP
SHE'S A HACKER TOO, THAT CHIHARU.
SHE FIDDLED WITH THE COMPUTER SETTINGS FOR THE FERRIS WHEEL AND MADE IT STOP.
I DOUBT THE STAFF HERE HAS THE KNOW-HOW TO FIX IT.
THIS IS UNFORGIVABLE.
THERE MUST BE SOME-THING I CAN DO.

I KNOW YOU'RE ANGRY ...
...BUT RIGHT NOW, YOU NEED TO DO WHAT I SAY.
I KNOW THAT AT A TIME LIKE THIS...
...CALLING DAISY FOR HELP IS THE ONLY THING YOU'RE CAPABLE OF.
BUT CHIHARU KNOWS ABOUT DAISY TOO.
AND HE'LL NEED THE RIGHT PASSWORD TO ACCESS THE PROGRAM SHE SET.
SNAP
DAISY MAY BE A GENIUS, BUT HE'S DOESN'T HAVE A CHANCE UNLESS HE KNOWS WHAT IT IS.
THE PASSWORD IS IN THIS MESSAGE.
Unsent Messages
You have an unsent message. Send it now?
ALL I HAVE TO DO IS SEND IT TO HIM.
WHETHER IT GETS TO DAISY OR NOT...
...IS COM-PLETELY UP TO YOU.

ALL YOU HAVE TO DO IS TELL ME...
...WHO DAISY IS.
Help!
Waah Waah!
YOU DID ALL THIS...
...JUST TO FIND THAT OUT?
WELL, WE HAVE PLENTY OF THINGS GOING ON...
...BUT DAISY KEEPS INTERFERING.
YOUR SELLING HIM OUT WILL HIT HIM HARD.
THIS JUST HAPPENS TO BE THE PERFECT OPPORTUNITY.
YOU'RE ABOUT TO FIND OUT DAISY'S PAST...
...AND YOU'RE GOING TO ABANDON HIM.
WH...

WHAT DO YOU MEAN BY THAT?!
WHAT DO YOU KNOW ABOUT DAISY...?
SHUP
ONLY I GET TO ASK THE QUESTIONS HERE. TELL ME WHAT I WANT TO KNOW.
HEY, STOP. STOP.
IF YOU DON'T, I'M GONNA DELETE THIS MESSAGE...
...IN TEN SECONDS.
NINE.
EIGHT.
SEVEN... SPEAK NOW OR FOREVER HOLD YOUR PEACE.
REMEMBER, THERE ARE INNOCENT PEOPLE INVOLVED.
FIVE.
FOUR.
TOO BAD ABOUT THE PASSWORD...
TWO.
ONE.
CHAK
WAIT.

DAISY IS ACTUALLY...
I'M SORRY, DAISY.
...THERE.
I'M SO SORRY.
YOU MUST BE SO WORRIED RIGHT NOW.
IN ORDER TO SAVE MYSELF AND THE OTHERS...
...I HAVE TO DO THIS...
I DIDN'T HEAR THE CRUCIAL PART.
REPEAT WHAT YOU SAID.
DAISY IS ACTUALLY...
... THERE.
Turn this way.
GEEZ... I CAN'T HEAR YOU.
I KNOW YOU DON'T WANT TO TELL ME, BUT...
I SAID...
I REALLY HAVE NO OTHER CHOICE...
DAISY IS ACTUALLY...

...A PRETTY FLOWER!!
...BUT TO MUSTER UP EVERY OUNCE OF MY STRENGTH.
EVEN I...
...CAN PROTECT...
...THE ONE I CHERISH.
NO MATTER WHAT HAPPENS...
CHAK
...I COULD NEVER...

...EVER...
...BETRAY ...
...THE ONE I LOVE.
DOOT
Message Sent
HUF
HUF
HA HA...
I... I GOT IT...
HEH HEH...
I WIN.
IT'S YOUR FAULT FOR BEING FOOLED.
Actually, everything is your fault.
NOW, YOUR SCHEME—
I JUST SENT THE MESSAGE. SO THERE!
HEE HEE...

HYA HA HA HA HA HA HA HA HA HA HA!
THIS IS SO INSANE.
WHO WOULD HAVE THOUGHT YOU'D SEND IT YOURSELF?
DID YOU REALLY BELIEVE WHAT I SAID ABOUT A PASSWORD?
TAKE A LOOK AT THE MESSAGE YOU JUST SENT.
DOOT
Sent Messages
Daisy
Daisy
Haruka
Daisy
CHIHARU COMPOSED IT...
...BUT SHE WROTE IT AS THOUGH YOU WERE THE SENDER.
CRAZY, HUH? IT SOUNDS LIKE IT CAME FROM YOU.

IF YOU LEARNED DAISY'S SECRET...
...SHE FIGURED THIS IS WHAT YOU MIGHT SAY.
y
n't forgive
u for killing
ny brother.
Please just
disappear
from my life.
WITH THIS, WE'LL KNOW WHO DAISY REALLY IS...
...THE POOR DESPONDENT GUY READING THIS MESSAGE RIGHT NOW.

BEEP
Please stay back.
Daisy
I can't forgive you for killing my brother.
Please just disappear from my life.
BUMP
IT'S NO USE! THE FERRIS WHEEL ISN'T MOVING.
CALL THE FIRE DEPARTMENT! WE NEED A FIRE ENGINE!!
No, we can't take matters into our own hands.
Why not? What about the people up there?
YOO-HOO...
HEY, BLONDIE.

HOW COME YOU'RE ALL ALONE, LOOKING SO SAD?
DID YOU GET DITCHED? OR ARE YOU LOST?
OH MY, LOOK AT THOSE LIFELESS EYES.
SOMETHING SAD MUST'VE HAPPENED.
I'LL MAKE YOU FEEL BETTER, IF YOU LIKE.
AH...
I'M CHIHARU. CHIHARU MORI.
IT'S BEEN A LONG TIME, DAISY.
...DID YOU GET PLASTIC SURGERY?
Your face looks different.
HOW RUDE. I JUST CHANGED MY HAIRSTYLE AND MAKEUP.
NEVER MIND THAT. DON'T YOU HAVE SOMETHING ELSE YOU WANT TO SAY TO ME?
You're so dense.

*CRACK - TO HACK INTO A COMPUTER PROGRAM.

IF YOU STILL WANT TO SAVE THAT GIRL...
...FOLLOW ME.
DON'T LOOK LIKE THAT, TERU.
ARE YOU IN SHOCK?
WELL, I'M NOT GONNA APOLOGIZE.
I FEEL BAD FOR YOU, BUT YOU ONLY HAVE YOURSELF TO BLAME.
You said the same thing earlier.
YOU SENT THE MESSAGE, SO THERE'S NOTHING YOU CAN DO NOW.

BESIDES, WHY SHOULD THE MESSAGE BOTHER YOU?
IT'S TRUE. DAISY DID KILL YOUR BROTHER.
Daisy
I can't forgive you for killing my brother.
Please just disapp
from my life.
TWITCH
NHN ...!!
WHAP
WHOA... THAT WAS CLOSE.
HEE HEE. FINALLY. A REACTION.
Can I have your bag?
IT'S NO FUN WHEN YOU'RE QUIET. SPAR WITH ME.
WILL YOU QUIT JOKING AROUND?! AND DON'T LIE!

DENGEKI DAISY
QUESTION CORNER

BALDLY ASK!!

Q.
PLEASE TELL ME WHAT KUROSAKI THINKS IS A SUREFIRE WAY TO WIN LOVE. ♡♡

(A.M., AICHI PREFECTURE)

A.
...ACTUALLY, WILL YOU TEACH THAT IDIOT? (I BEG YOU.) I MEAN, YOU CAN'T TRUST KUROSAKI WHEN IT COMES TO LOVE. SERIOUSLY, ARE YOU REALLY A 24-YEAR-OLD GROWN-UP, YOU IDIOT?!!

Q.
DO THE CHARACTERS WHO APPEAR REGULARLY IN *DENGEKI DAISY* LIKE TO BATHE?
ALSO, WHERE DO THEY WASH FIRST?

(A.A., TOYAMA PREFECTURE)

A.
EVERYBODY LOVES TO BATHE (EXCEPT SOICHIRO).
EVERYONE BEGINS BY WASHING THEIR HAIR. AND NEXT:

- TERU – LEFT ARM (IT'S THE OPPOSITE OF HER GOOD ARM.)
- KUROSAKI – THE BACK OF HIS NECK (WASHES FROM TOP TO BOTTOM)
- RIKO – TOES (STARTS WITH HARD-TO-REACH SPOTS)
- SOICHIRO – STINKY PLACES FIRST (WASHING TAKES AWAY THE ODOR)

A FEW MORE TIDBITS...

- KUROSAKI LIKES BATH SALTS THAT TURN THE WATER A MILKY COLOR.
- TERU YEARNS TO TAKE BUBBLE BATHS BUT HAS NEVER EXPERIENCED THEM BEFORE.
- RIKO TAKES HIP BATHS TWICE A WEEK.
- SOICHIRO SINGS A LOT IN THE BATH.

THAT'S ABOUT IT.

MY EDITOR AND I CAME UP WITH THE ABOVE INFORMATION.
THE EDITOR SAID, "INFORMATION ABOUT HOW KIYOSHI BATHES IS TOTALLY BORING!" IT SEEMS THAT BOSS AND DIRECTOR WEREN'T EVEN ON THE LIST! HOW MEAN! BUT THE EDITOR IS FAIR!!

THAT'S IT FOR THIS VOLUME. AND NOT A SINGLE BALDIE JOKE (SHOCK)!!!

MY BROTHER DIED IN THE HOSPITAL FROM AN ILLNESS!
DAISY COULDN'T HAVE KILLED MY BROTHER! THAT'S AN OUTRIGHT LIE!!
HM?
WHY DO YOU KEEP VILIFYING DAISY?
OH, I SHOULD CLARIFY.
I GUESS "KILLED" MAY NOT BE QUITE THE RIGHT WORD.
I SHOULD HAVE SAID, "IT WAS DAISY'S FAULT THAT YOUR BROTHER DIED."
THAT'S MORE SPECIFIC, RIGHT?

DAISY CREATED SOMETHING EXTREMELY DANGEROUS...
...SO HE GOT INTO SOME SERIOUS TROUBLE.
YOUR BROTHER BECAME EMBROILED IN IT...
...AND HE ENDED UP DYING FROM EXHAUSTION.
ANYWAY, DAISY PRETTY MUCH CAUSED HIS DEATH.
YOU'RE PROBABLY THINKING THE SAME THING, RIGHT?
HE'S THE ONE YOU SHOULD BE MAD AT. NOT ME.
THIS COULD BE TRUE...
BY THE TIME SOICHIRO WAS HOSPITALIZED, IT WAS FAR TOO LATE.
HE ONLY HAD A FEW WEEKS LEFT.

NO WONDER...
...DAISY COULDN'T TELL ME...
...AND WAS IN SUCH PAIN.
AND...
...HE FINALLY MADE UP HIS MIND...
...TO TELL ME TODAY...
Daisy
I can't forgive you for
killing my brother.
Please just disappear
from my life.
I'LL JUST BET DAISY...
...KEPT TELLING HIMSELF THINGS LIKE, "PLEASE DON'T LET TERU FIND OUT.
"PLEASE DON'T LET HER KNOW."

DAISY, IT'S NOT TRUE.
BUT YOU SENT HIM THAT MESSAGE.
IT'S A LIE.
I MUST...
...DO SOMETHING...
IT'S TOO LATE NOW. YOU CAN'T TAKE IT BACK.
THERE'S NOTHING YOU CAN DO FROM UP HERE.
STOP.
REALLY...
YOU SHOULDN'T HAVE PULLED THAT STUNT EARLIER, SEE?
PLEASE STOP.

MY MIND IS A BLANK.
HELP ME.
DAISY WON'T COME BACK ANYMORE.
FORGET ABOUT HIM.
CLOSED FOR CLEANING
IT'S ALL RIGHT. NO ONE'S COMING, SO RELAX.
ARE YOU KIDDING ME?
Wanna smoke?
This is a non-smoking area. Put it out, will you?
I DON'T CARE IF I'M ARRESTED. I JUST DON'T WANT IT TO BE FOR CRIMINAL INDECENCY.
*ENTERING THE RESTROOM OF THE OPPOSITE SEX SEEMS TO BE A MISDEMEANOR.
IF YOU HAVE SOME-THING TO SAY, JUST GET TO THE POINT.
IT'S QUITE JUICY.

THE SECRET VIRUS CALLED "JACK FROST."
IF YOU HEARD A RUMOR THAT IT STILL EXISTS...
...WHAT WOULD YOU DO?
YES.
THE VIRUS THAT TOOK THE LIFE OF THAT GIRL'S BROTHER, SOICHIRO.
THE SOURCE OF DAISY'S GUILT.

WELL? DON'T YOU FIND THAT INTEREST-ING?
WANT TO KNOW MORE?
KRII
YOU KNOW I DO.
HOW DO I GET YOU TO TELL ME THE DETAILS?
HEH HEH... NOW THAT'S WHAT I LIKE.
LEAN
DO YOU REMEMBER WHAT I ONCE SAID TO YOU?
ABOUT SERVING ANOTHER PRINCESS?
HA HA... DID YOU SAY THAT?
AY ANY RATE...
...YOU CAN'T GO BACK TO THE OTHER PRINCESS NOW.
HEY...
YOU SHOULD REMEMBER TOO.

GASP...
AH...
H-HOW DARE YOU LAY... A HAND... ON A WOMAN...
Stop...
I DON'T KNOW WHAT YOU'RE UP TO, BUT IF YOU WANT ME TO DANCE, I'LL DANCE.
DIDN'T I TELL YOU THERE'S NO TELLING WHAT A LOYAL SERVANT WILL DO?
SO IF YOU HAVE INFORMATION, SPIT IT OUT.
BUT LET ME MAKE ONE THING CLEAR.
I'VE ALREADY SWORN TO SERVE MY PRINCESS FOR THE REST OF MY LIFE.

WHETHER I CAN GO BACK TO HER OR NOT...
...DOESN'T MATTER.
RING
TWITCH
OH, IT'S CHIHARU.
MAN, WHAT TIMING...
SHE'S PROBABLY GETTING CHUMMY WITH DAISY AS WE SPEAK.
HELLO?

HEY, CHIHARU. HOW'D IT GO? DID IT WORK?
NEVER MIND THAT. SHUT UP AND LISTEN!!
THE FERRIS WHEEL IS TURNING BACK ON. MY PLAN WENT AWRY.
I GAVE YOU THE STUN GUN AS A PRECAUTION, REMEMBER? USE IT AND GET AWAY BY YOURSELF!!
What...?
BUT WHY? YOU SAID YOU'D COME FOR US.
WHERE ARE YOU, CHIHARU?
HUH? BUY CLOTHES? WHAT CLOTHES? WHERE'S DAISY...?
Dammit! I can't do a thing while I'm like this!
HE TOOK EVERYTHING! MY LAPTOP, MY CLOTHES, EVERYTHING!
KEEP THE RESTROOM
DAISY'LL BE ABLE TO FIGURE OUT WHAT I DID IN AN INSTANT.
WHAT? DAISY'S FIXING THE FERRIS WHEEL RIGHT NOW?
HOW? IS HE...?
HUH...?

DAISY...?
TAP...
WRR...
WRR...
BEEP...
OH...
IT'S A MESSAGE.
DAISY

IT'S LIKE THE KIND I ALWAYS GET...
FROM KIND...
...DAISY...
Daisy
Teru, I'm sorry.
You must have been so scared.
I turned the Ferris Wheel back on
now, so there's no need to
I don't think you wrote
I received.
I KNEW IT.
worry. I don't
that message I rece
But it's true that I killed you
beloved brother. I know it's
unforgivable. I'm a coward for
leaving you after hurting you
like this. Go ahead and hate
me. Thank you for pretending
not to know who I am.

BANG
The Ferris Wheel is moving again!
RINNG...
TRASH
RINNNG
RINNG
TERU, I'M SORRY.
RINNG...
RINNG...
IT'S TRUE THAT I KILLED YOUR BELOVED BROTHER.

I KNOW IT'S UNFORGIVABLE.

KUROSAKI! KUROSAKI!!
PLEASE ANSWER YOUR PHONE!!

I'M A COWARD FOR LEAVING YOU AFTER HURTING YOU LIKE THIS.

THAT MESSAGE WAS FAKE! IT WASN'T FROM ME!
IF ONLY I HAD...
...TOLD HIM EARLIER...
DO YOU HEAR WHAT I'M SAYING? YOU DON'T HAVE TO GO AWAY!!

GO AHEAD AND HATE ME.

I DON'T UNDER-STAND WHY YOU CAN'T BE FORGIVEN.
WHY...?
AND I DON'T UNDER-STAND WHAT HURT YOU CAUSED ME!!

MOVE THIS FERRIS WHEEL FASTER!! PLEASE!!
BANG BANG BANG
DAISY IS GOING TO LEAVE!! HURRY!!
WHY COULDN'T I DO IT?
DON'T GO, DAISY! DON'T GO!!
PLEASE DON'T...
CLAK...
THANK YOU FOR PRETENDING NOT TO KNOW WHO I AM.

THANK YOU FOR ALWAYS SMILING WHEN YOU WERE AROUND ME.

YOU ALWAYS HAD A CUTE WAY OF PUTTING UP WITH MY RUDENESS. THANK YOU.

...HOW YOU LOVE DAISIES...
I CAME TO APPRECIATE THEM TOO.

BUT I THINK THE GIRL WHO WAS NEAR ME...

...WAS FAR MORE BEAUTIFUL...

...THAN THAT FLOWER.

DENGEKI DAISY 7 *THE END*

AFTERWORD

One-day Pass
Adult 3000 yen
Child 1500 yen
Seniors 2000 yen
Couples (2 tickets)
5000 yen
Two adults tickets... Th-the Couples discount kind...
5000
Maybe I should have pinned back my hair.
But I used a smooth-hair treatment yesterday...
AMUSEMENT PARK TICKET OFFICE

...UM. YEAH. THAT'S IT FOR *DENGEKI DAISY* VOLUME 7.
WHAT CAN I SAY? ...I APOLOGIZE THAT THIS TURNED OUT TO HAVE SO MANY SUPER GO-BALD-KUROSAKI STORY TWISTS. ESPECIALLY WHEN THIS IS THE SEVENTH VOLUME (LUCKY 7).
DESPITE IT ALL, *DENGEKI DAISY* IS STILL BEING SERIALIZED IN *BETSUCOMI*. IF THINGS GO WELL, THEY MAY ALLOW AN EIGHTH VOLUME. SO I'M GOING TO DO MY BEST! THINGS ARE BEGINNING TO UNFOLD IN STARK FASHION, AND FOR THE AUTHOR, THE PRESSURE IS ON MORE THAN EVER. BUT I HOPE THAT ALL OF YOU WILL LOOK FORWARD TO THE NEXT VOLUME. PLEASE DON'T FORSAKE ME. I MEAN, *DENGEKI DAISY* **IS NOT A SERIOUS MANGA AT ALL. IT'S JUST A "HEH HEH HEH" MANGA ABOUT A PERVERTED GUY WHO HAS A LOLITA COMPLEX.**

SO, IF YOU SENSED ANY SUSPENSE IN THE STORY, BELIEVE ME, IT'S JUST YOUR IMAGINATION. THAT BLEACHED BLOND PUNK WILL BE TEASED MERCILESSLY INTO LOSING HIS HAIR IN NO TIME. NOT TO MENTION THE STORY WILL GO BACK TO HIM SITTING COZILY AND FLIRTING WITH A CERTAIN YOUNG GIRL.

SO, PLEASE BE PATIENT AND WAIT A LITTLE BIT MORE.

KYOUSUKE MOTOMI
最富 キョウスケ

DENGEKI DAISY
"BALDLY ASK!!" CORNER
C/O DENGEKI DAISY EDITOR
VIZ MEDIA
P.O. BOX 77010
SAN FRANCISCO, CA 94107

← IF YOU HAVE ANY QUESTIONS FOR THE QUESTION CORNER, PLEASE SEND THEM HERE.
FOR REGULAR FAN MAIL, PLEASE SEND THEM TO THE SAME ADDRESS BUT CHANGE THE ADDRESSEE TO:

KYOUSUKE MOTOMI
C/O DENGEKI DAISY EDITOR

...AND THAT'S IT. THANK YOU VERY MUCH!!

Dear TAKU. You always made our family more peaceful. So, we'll make sure to be with you forever.

I got myself a new wallet. (Geez, is that all I have to talk about?) Anyway, I got all excited and chose this super-refined wallet made in the true, traditional Japanese style. It's quite cool. But there's only sixty yen in it right now.

-Kyousuke Motomi

Born on August 1, Kyousuke Motomi debuted in *Deluxe Betsucomi* with *Hetakuso Kyupiddo* (No-Good Cupid) in 2002. She is the creator of *Otokomae! Biizu Kurabu* (Handsome! Beads Club), and her latest work, *Dengeki Daisy,* is currently being serialized in *Betsucomi.* Motomi enjoys sleeping, tea ceremonies and reading Haruki Murakami.

DENGEKI DAISY
VOL. 7
Shojo Beat Edition

STORY AND ART BY
KYOUSUKE MOTOMI

Original Japanese edition "DENGEKI DAISY"
published by SHOGAKUKAN Inc.

Translation & Adaptation/JN Productions
Touch-up Art & Lettering/Rina Mapa
Design/Nozomi Akashi
Editor/Amy Yu

Printed in the U.S.A.

Published by VIZ Media, LLC
P.O. Box 77010
San Francisco, CA 94107

10 9 8 7 6 5 4 3 2 1
First printing, November 2011

www.viz.com

www.shojobeat.com

PARENTAL ADVISORY
DENGEKI DAISY is rated T+ for Older Teen and is recommended for ages 16 and up. This volume contains suggestive themes.
ratings.viz.com